The Candida Albicans Yeast-Free Cookbook

OTHER KEATS TITLES OF INTEREST

The
CANDIDA ALBICANS
Yeast-Free
COOKBOOK

PAT CONNOLLY

and

ASSOCIATES OF THE PRICE-POTTENGER
NUTRITION FOUNDATION

KEATS PUBLISHING, INC.   NEW CANAAN, CONNECTICUT

The information in this book is not intended as medical advice. Its intention is solely informational and educational. It is assumed that the reader will consult a medical or health professional should the need for one be warranted.

Library of Congress Cataloging in Publication Data

Connolly, Pat.
   The Candida albicans yeast-free cookbook.

   Bibliography: p.
   Includes index.
   1. Candidiasis—Prevention. 2. Candidiasis—Diet therapy—Recipes. 3. Yeast-free diet—Recipes. 4. Sugar-free diet—Recipes. 5. Candida albicans. I. Price-Pottenger Nutrition Foundation. II. Title.
RC123.C3C66 1985   641.5′631   85-9730
ISBN 0-87983-409-9

Printed in the United States of America

Keats Publishing, Inc., 27 Pine Street (Box 876) New Canaan, Connecticut 06840

Contents

About PPNF

The Price-Pottenger Nutrition Foundation is dedicated to the principle that the quality of our soil and the health and well-being of our plant and animal kingdoms determine the physical foundation of human life, which in turn promotes balanced mental and spiritual being.

In keeping with the spirit of its two great nutritional pioneers, Drs. Weston A. Price and Francis Pottenger, Jr., PPNF acts as a nation-wide clearing house for current health information. The goal of the dedicated staff is to promote public awareness of the importance of good nutrition by means of educational publications, research and demonstrations. The desire to help the more than 100,000 individuals requesting information about Candida albicans helped this cookbook become a reality.

The work of the Foundation is made possible by the international membership of health professionals and lay persons who contribute both informatively and monetarily. The many readers of the *Candida Cookbook* are invited to participate in the activities of the Foundation by contributing original recipes to the PPNF journal. For information on membership in the Foundation and to receive current journals, send a stamped self-addressed envelope to **PPNF, PO Box 2614, La Mesa, CA 92041.**

ACKNOWLEDGMENTS

We wish to thank the many who helped to make this book possible:

The Candida patients who insisted on dietary help in book form

Shirley Lorenzani who first told us of the yeast problem

Bruce Pacetti who refined Price and Page dietary ideas into the Rainbow Meal Plan

Beatrice Trum Hunter, our editor, who shaped the book into readable form

An Keats, whose patience and help made her a joy to work with

Mary Marston, who experienced the diet, wrote detailed instructions for us, and researched, tested and rewrote recipes

Nancy Kelly who kept us going day after day and pulled it all together

Arthur Mitchell who brought us reference cookbooks at critical times

William C. Crook, M.D., who cheerfully gave us valuable advice

C. Orian Truss, M.D., and his team of hundreds of physicians who are showing us how to regain our health

Helen Fahrney, who tasted, made suggestions and tasted again

Introduction

Do you feel bad all over? Are you bothered with fatigue, headache, depression, irritability and memory loss? Or do you suffer symptoms caused by disturbances in your reproductive organs, including prostatitis, loss of sexual interest and/or impotence, premenstrual tension, menstrual irregularities, persistent vaginitis, endometriosis or infertility?

Are you troubled with digestive symptoms, sore muscles and joints, multiple sclerosis, chronic hives, psoriasis (or other skin problems) or mitral valve prolapse? If your answer is "yes" to any of these questions and if you've taken a lot of antibiotics, birth control pills or corticosteroids, chances are that your health problems are related to the common and usually benign yeast, Candida albicans.

For centuries this yeast has been known to cause vaginal problems and skin and mouth rashes. However, not until the brilliant pioneer observations of C. Orian Truss, M.D. did physicians (or anyone else) realize that this usually "benign critter" could play an important part in causing so many health problems.

Some twenty-three years ago, Truss, a Birmingham, Alabama internist and allergist, first noted that Candida albicans made several of his patients sick. During the next sixteen years he saw many other patients whose illnesses were related to yeasts. He reported his findings in a series of four articles in the *Journal of Orthomolecular Psychiatry* beginning in 1978. Yet prior to 1982 only a handful of physicians had learned of his observations.

Then, beginning in 1982, word of the yeast-human relationship began to spread. Now, in 1985 hundreds of physicians and tens of thousands of yeast victims are learning about yeast-connected health disorders.

I first became aware of the Truss work in 1979 and during the past five years I've seen hundreds of patients respond to anti-fungal medication and a sugar-free, yeast-free diet.

You are what you eat, and eating really nutritious food is your most important requirement for good health. Yet in America today you're constantly encouraged by television, magazine and newspaper advertisements to eat processed, sweetened, colored, refined foods. Moreover, some nutrition "authorities" even endorse the consumption of such foods.

But there are dissenting voices—courageous, knowledgeable and articulate individuals who are "telling it like it is" and working to bring sound nutritional knowledge to all who would listen. One such individual is Pat Connolly, Curator of the Price-Pottenger Nutrition Foundation. During the past decade I've learned a lot from Mrs. Connolly's clinical observations and the publications of the Price-Pottenger Foundation.

If you're bothered by yeast-connected health problems, you'll need the help, support, encouragement and supervision of an experienced and interested physician and other health professionals to prescribe antifungal medication and supervise your overall treatment program. Equally important you'll need to consume a well-balanced, nutritious diet composed of foods that do not encourage yeast growth.

Yeasts thrive on carbohydrates, especially foods which contain sugar (sucrose, glucose, and fructose). Accordingly, you'll need to avoid all foods containing table sugar and refined forms of sucrose, glucose and fructose. In addition, during the initial weeks on your diet you'll need to avoid fruits and you may also need to avoid the high-carbohydrate grains, especially those which contain gluten. You'll also need to avoid mushrooms, cheeses and other yeast-containing foods since many individuals with yeast-related health problems experience allergic reactions when they eat these foods. As your immune system improves and the Candida in your digestive tract is brought under control, your diet can usually be expanded.

In *The Candida Albicans Yeast-Free Cookbook*, you are provided with a dietary program which has been found to be highly effective in bringing Candida overgrowth in the digestive tract under control. Featured in the book are many recipes which will help you maintain an adequate nutritional state while starving the Candida organisms which live in your digestive tract. Although, the initial phases of the program are rigorous and demanding, as you improve you can usually return some of these forbidden foods to your diet, including the complex carbohydrates.

Bringing a yeast-connected health disorder under control and regaining your health won't be easy. It usually requires months and years of patient, consistent work. This book should help you significantly in regaining your health.

William G. Crook, M.D.

Foreword

Several health problems have burgeoned that appear to be induced by factors in our radical transformation of lifestyle that has occurred in the twentieth century. Though disparate, these health problems all seem to be related to imbalances in the body, created by the replacement of novelty foods for traditional ones. We are all participants—with neither knowledge nor consent—to an experiment on an unprecedented scale in the history of humankind. We are eating foods that have been radically altered through various processes of refining, heating, pressurizing and chemical manipulation. As a result, the food has been disrupted in all classifications of known essential nutrients. The state of the art in food processing has reached a highly sophisticated level. The total sum of the numerous nutrient deficits it produces, and their interconnections, are difficult to identify. Twentieth-century changes in lifestyle, including urbanization, increased use of new medications, alcohol, tobacco, drugs and other factors, further complicate this disruption. There is a glimmer of awareness that some diseases that have become major health problems in recent times, including cardiovascular diseases, cancer and schizophrenia, seem to be related to dietary alterations.

Candida albicans, quite recently identified as a surprisingly widespread yeast infection, fits this paradigm. The yeast, normally held in check within the healthy body, is out of control and proliferates when the body is in a state of imbalance. Candida albicans appears to be a twentieth-century problem of epidemic proportions caused by several aspects of the radical transformation of food and lifestyle.

Antibiotics, developed in this century, have become widely used. They are not only administered as medication, but they also appear in many foods as residue, resulting from their use with food animals. Repeated exposures to low levels of antibiotics have succeeded in destroying the beneficial organisms within the human body that normally keep Candida in check.

Another factor has been the introduction of "the Pill," and its widespread use by many women.

Steroids, chemical therapies and numerous drugs which act as immunosuppressants weaken the body's ability to maintain balance.

Another opportunity to imbalance the body was provided

by changed dietary patterns, with increased consumption of simple carbohydrates (refined flours and sugar) at the expense of complex carbohydrates (such as wholegrains or potatoes).

Imbalance in the body, induced by Candida, can be manifested in various organs, tissues, systems and functions. It may affect the gastrointestinal tract, with symptoms of indigestion, food cravings or food allergies. Or it may affect the central nervous system with resultant numbness or tingling. The structure of the body may be affected by joint pains and stiffness. The circulatory system may be impaired, manifested by cold hands and feet. The emotions may be affected, ranging from feelings of fatigue, depression or premenstrual tension to a loss of libido. Hormones may malfunction, and result in symptoms running the gamut from acne or dry rough skin to menstrual disturbances and miscarriage.

Fortunately, once the Candida problem is identified, it is possible for the individual to embark on a program to restore the body's balance. Dietary measures are crucial in the control of Candida. While identification of Candida probably is best done by a health professional, the restoration of health is largely in the hands of the individual Candida sufferer. This cookbook will serve as a reliable guide to help restore the state of balance.

The Rainbow Meal Plan suggested in this cookbook has a good record of helpfulness when used by individuals suffering from a variety of health problems, especially those of fungal origin. The plan can be applied to Candida as well. The Rainbow Meal Plan offers good nutrition to the body, but at the same time, starves the Candida. The underlying principles include traditional food and avoid novelty ones. Hence, it is reversing the long path down which we have been led in the twentieth century, to our detriment. The Modified Meal Plan, a less stringent program than the Rainbow, simply eliminates foods and preparation methods that encourage Candida. The recipes follow these rules without sacrificing nutrition or pleasant eating. When faithfully followed, these plans offer hope and restorative possibilities. The ultimate goal is not only to control Candida albicans but to balance the body systems properly. With that achievement, good health benefits flow.

Beatrice Trum Hunter

Preface

The recognition in recent years of Candida albicans by major medical authorities is finally coinciding with patient histories of "feeling below par" and "unable to cope" syndromes accompanied by discomfort and distress.

If you have purchased this book, you are no doubt already somewhat familiar with the growing amount of literature on the subject of Candida. You have probably committed yourself to a treatment plan that includes a dietary regimen which will lead to improved spirits and restored health.

A restrictive diet need not be a sacrifice. Many persons who have tried one of the Candida control diet plans for several months or even weeks find that it is quite satisfying. The program controls not only Candida, but also related problems such as overweight and food cravings.

Candida albicans is one of many microorganisms that normally lives in the gastrointestinal tract. In the healthy person, its presence is not a problem. When it goes out of control and proliferates, however, it can eventually damage the GI tract and spread into other organs and tissues of the body. This sequence can cause a variety of unpleasant symptoms.

This overgrowth of yeast and all of its troublesome bodily manifestations can be treated successfully. By adhering to a restrictive diet and, for some, using an antifungal drug such as nystatin under a physician's guidance, the Candida overgrowth can be controlled in most cases and the annoying symptoms will be reduced or eliminated.

Dietary restrictions are an essential part of the Candida treatment plan. The comprehensive *Candida Albicans Yeast-Free Cookbook* has been developed by the Price-Pottenger Nutrition Foundation in San Diego, California, to make the permissible nutritious foods as appetizing and delectable as possible while the healing process is progressing.

*This book is dedicated to those who
taught us how we should eat:*

WESTON A. PRICE, D.D.S.
FRANCIS M. POTTENGER, JR., M.D.
MELVIN PAGE, D.D.S.
ALFREDA ROOKE, M.P.H.
THE HEALTHY PRIMITIVES
BRUCE PACETTI, D.D.S.
JOSEPH CONNOLLY, JR., D.D.S.

The Candida Albicans Yeast-Free Cookbook

Do You Have Candida Albicans? A Questionnaire

The remarkable recovery of many patients suffering from the symptoms associated with Candida albicans and the development of this cookbook, are mainly due to the efforts of two medical doctors who have persisted courageously in research that has brought Candida albicans to the forefront of current medical issues. C. Orian Truss, M. D., of Birmingham, Alabama and Sidney M. Baker, M.D., of The Gesell Institute of Human Behavior, New Haven, Connecticut, are recognized pioneers in current research and clinical observations of yeast-connected illnesses.

In his enlightening book, *The Missing Diagnosis*, Dr. Truss cites numerous cases of misdiagnosed, untreated Candida patients who were often stigmatized as psychosomatics.[1] According to Dr. Truss, "Candida albicans is in everyone and it is readily apparent that its presence is entirely compatible with a lifetime of excellent health. It is equally apparent, however, that under the influence of various factors, it may successfully invade and colonize mucous membranes, skin and nails. . . . Such infections may be acute, brief and intermittent."

Truss's work is of major significance in that he has documented histories of patients with a wide spectrum of symptoms who have drastically improved or completely recovered under his treatment program for Candida, which includes dietary restraints and often the use of nystatin.

He cautions, however, that these remarkable recoveries may in fact be related to some aspect of the treatment plan other than the "die-off" of the fungi. "Even should Candida be unrelated etiologically, patients with an autoimmune disease deserve to have their yeast problems treated. If it is not the cause of their illness, treating it should do no harm, and if it is the cause, then that is what we are looking for," Truss concluded in his paper, "The Role of Candida Albicans in Human Illness."[2]

With the growing awareness of Candida as a systemic illness that plays a significant role in health, the question arises:

Why has it not been discussed in medical journals for so long? Dr. Truss believes that there are two reasons. At present, definitive tests are nonexistent for identification of Candida as a causative indicator, since it is present in most individuals and is often categorized as an "opportunistic organism." Also, what Dr. Truss calls the "psychosomatic complex" has provided a safety valve for doctors who attempt to diagnose patients' complaints that have no clearly discernible cause.

According to Dr. Truss, the proliferation of broad-spectrum antibiotics following World War II and, later, the widespread use of both birth control pills and cortisone-type steroids, combined with increasingly high-carbohydrate diets, has culminated in numerous yeast-related illnesses. He suggests that current problems, including drug abuse, behavioral disorders, and suicide among young people, may be related to an inefficiently functioning immune system and the consequences of Candida albicans overgrowth.

In recent years, medical researchers of Candida albicans-related syndromes have pooled their findings at several national conferences. At the Yeast-Human-Interaction Conference in November 1983, Drs. Truss and Baker were featured speakers.

The Yeast Connection: A Medical Breakthrough, by William G. Crook, M.D., published in 1983, is a guidebook for patients and the general public that provides a better understanding of the implications and complications in diagnosis and treatment of Candida albicans.[3]

The following questionnaire, designed by Dr. Crook, provides a list of the symptoms and medical histories that might indicate the presence of Candida overgrowth. The variety of symptoms, however, suggests the importance of making the diagnosis with a physician's guidance.

Candida Questionnaire and Score Sheet

This questionnaire is designed for adults and is not appropriate for children. It lists factors in your medical history that promote the growth of Candida albicans (Section A), and symptoms commonly found in individuals with yeast-connected illnesses (Sections B and C).

For each "Yes" answer in Section A, circle the Point Score in that section. Total your score and record it in the box at the end of the section. Then move on to Sections B and C and score as directed.

Filling out and scoring this questionnaire should help you and your physician evaluate the possible role of Candida in contributing to your health problem, but it will not provide an absolute "Yes" or "No" answer.

SECTION A: HISTORY   **POINT SCORE**

1. Have you taken tetracylines (Sumycin®, Panmycin®, Vibramycin®, Minocin®, etc.) or other antibiotics for acne for 1 month (or longer)?   35

2. Have you, at any time in your life, taken other "broad-spectrum" antibiotics† for respiratory, urinary or other infections (for 2 months or longer, or in shorter courses 4 or more times in a 1-year period)?   35

3. Have you taken a broad-spectrum antibiotic drug†—even a single course?   6

4. Have you, at any time in your life, been bothered by persistent prostatitis, vaginitis or other problems affecting your reproductive organs?   25

5. Have you been pregnant . . .
2 or more times?   5

1 time?   3

6. Have you taken birth control pills . . .
For more than 2 years?   15

For 6 months to 2 years?   8

7. Have you taken prednisone, Decadron® or other cortisone-type drugs . . .
For more than 2 weeks?   15

For 2 weeks or less?   6

8. Does exposure to perfumes, insecticides, fabric shop odors and other chemicals provoke . . .
Moderate to severe symptoms?   20

†Including Keflex®, ampicillin, amoxicillin, Ceclor®, Bactrim® and Septra®. Such antibiotics kill off "good germs" while they're killing off those which cause infection.

Mild symptoms?	5

9. Are your symptoms worse on damp, muggy days or in moldy places?   20

10. Have you had athlete's foot, ringworm, "jock itch" or other chronic fungous infections of the skin or nails? Have such infections been . . .

Severe or persistent?	20

Mild to moderate?	10

11. Do you crave sugar?	10

12. Do you crave breads?	10

13. Do you crave alcoholic beverages?	10

14. Does tobacco smoke *really* bother you?	10

TOTAL SCORE, SECTION A

SECTION B: MAJOR SYMPTOMS:

For each of your symptoms, enter the appropriate figure in the Point Score column:

If a symptom is *occasional or mild* ....score 3 points
If a symptom is *frequent and/or moderately severe* ...score 6 points
If a symptom is *severe and/or disabling* ....score 9 points
Add total score and record it in the box at the end of this section

POINT SCORE

1. Fatigue or lethargy

2. Feeling of being "drained"

3. Poor memory

4. Feeling "spacey" or "unreal"

5. Inability to make decisions

6. Numbness, burning or tingling

7. Insomnia

8. Muscle aches

9. Muscle weakness or paralysis

10. Pain and/or swelling in joints

11. Abdominal pain

12. Constipation

13. Diarrhea

14. Bloating, belching or intestinal gas

15. Troublesome vaginal burning, itching or discharge

16. Prostatitis

17. Impotence

18. Loss of sexual desire or feeling

19. Endometriosis or infertility

20. Cramps and/or other menstrual irregularities

21. Premenstrual tension

22. Attacks of anxiety or crying

23. Cold hands or feet and/or chilliness

24. Shaking or irritable when hungry

TOTAL SCORE, SECTION B

SECTION C: OTHER SYMPTOMS:†

For each of your symptoms, enter the appropriate figure in the Point Score column:

If a symptom is *occasional or mild* ....score 1 point

If a symptom is *frequent and/or moderately severe* ...score 2 points

If a symptom is *severe and/or disabling* ....score 3 points

Add total score and record it in the box at the end of this section.

POINT SCORE

1. Drowsiness

2. Irritability or jitteriness

3. Incoordination

4. Inability to concentrate

5. Frequent mood swings

6. Headache

7. Dizziness/loss of balance

8. Pressure above ears ... feeling of head swelling

9. Tendency to bruise easily

10. Chronic rashes or itching

11. Numbness, tingling

12. Indigestion or heartburn

13. Food sensitivity or intolerance

14. Mucus in stools

†While the symptoms in this section commonly occur in people with yeast-connected illness, they are also found in other individuals.

15. Rectal itching

16. Dry mouth or throat

17. Rash or blisters in mouth

18. Bad breath

19. Foot, hair or body odor not relieved by washing

20. Nasal congestion or post-nasal drip

21. Nasal itching

22. Sore throat

23. Laryngitis, loss of voice

24. Cough or recurrent bronchitis

25. Pain or tightness in chest

26. Wheezing or shortness of breath

27. Urinary urgency or frequency

28. Burning on urination

29. Spots in front of eyes or erratic vision

30. Burning or tearing of eyes

31. Recurrent infections or fluid in ears

32. Ear pain or deafness

TOTAL SCORE, SECTION C

TOTAL SCORE, SECTION A

TOTAL SCORE, SECTION B

GRAND TOTAL SCORE

The Grand Total Score will help you and your physician decide if your health problems are yeast-connected. Scores in women will run higher as 7 items in the questionnaire apply exclusively to women, while only 2 apply exclusively to men.

Yeast-connected health problems are almost certainly present in women with scores *over 180* and in men with scores *over 140*.

Yeast-connected health problems are probably present in women with scores *over 120* and in men with scores *over 90*.

Yeast-connected health problems are possibly present in women with scores *over 60* and in men with scores *over 40*.

With scores of less than 60 in women and 40 in men, yeasts are less apt to cause health problems.

LIVING WITH
CANDIDA ALBICANS

Shopping, Planning, and Using Leftovers

A fully effective diet for the treatment of Candida must not only starve the yeast, but provide all essential nutrients needed for the healing process. To promote adherence to the diet, meals should be satisfying, attractive, tasty and simple to prepare. The suggested diet is one that emphasizes a variety of vegetables and small amounts of protein; it also includes legumes and some grains. All foods should be fresh and whole. Conspicuously absent in the beginning of the program are fruits; honey; dairy products; seeds and nuts;* and yeasted and fermented foods. Although these are wholesome foods, they do not retard the growth of Candida.

Sugar in *any* form, including fruit, honey, molasses, maple syrup and all alcoholic beverages, makes Candida thrive and must be avoided. Since milk products contain milk sugar (lactose), all dairy foods except butter must also be omitted. Seeds and nuts are initially excluded because they are difficult to

---

*When symptoms abate, your doctor will reintroduce seeds and grains into the diet. Usually portions are restricted to ⅛ or ¼ cup of sprouted seeds or grains. Non-yeasted bread may be substituted in the same amount. Be sure to measure. If this amount is well tolerated, repeat again in four days. If no problems arise, add this amount of the new food to your diet. Use the same process of four-day testing for additional nuts and grains. Wait six weeks before repeating a test food if it is not well tolerated.

digest. They may be reinstated into the diet by trial and error experimentation at a later date.*

Yeast-containing foods, such as vinegar, mushrooms, yeasted breads, beer, wine and brewer's yeast must all be avoided. The Candida patient is already reacting to the Candida overgrowth in the body. Yeast-containing foods add an overload to the immune system, which is already functioning inefficiently.

Once you understand the simple basic principles of creating a yeast-free diet, you can enjoy attractive and nutritious meals that will help hasten your recovery from annoying chronic symptoms. Two varied and appetizing meal plans are presented to offer you satisfying meals and help you treat Candida effectively. The Rainbow Meal Plan is a clinically tested healing regimen for balancing the body's chemistry which is under stress from Candida and possibly from other factors.

The Modified Meal Plan is a collection of tested recipes that make use of the basic foods acceptable in an antifungal diet. You can choose the meal plan that best suits your needs and tastes. Or you can alternate plans while you work to restore your health and vigor.

Anti-Candida Shopping

For the yeast-free special diet or the yeast-free low-carbohydrate diet plans, supermarket shopping is easier than ever before. In general, you can bypass about 80 percent of the foods offered, and head directly to a few sections:

MEATS   Select fresh lean meats, poultry and fish. Avoid ground meat, pork, breaded and pickled meats, or any processed meat with additives. Some frozen food can be stored for convenience— for instance, keep a bag of frozen (unbreaded) scallops on hand. It's so easy to thaw a few for a quick meal, and reseal the package.

DAIRY PRODUCTS   Select fresh eggs and unsalted butter and ignore the rest. Look for the date on the egg cartons.

SEEDS, NUTS, LEGUMES AND GRAINS   These may be found in bulk packages. Be sure to use brown rice and whole grains.

PRODUCE   Pass up the fruit section. Select vegetables that look fresh and free of mold.

CONDIMENTS   Select olive oil, spices, herbs and sea salt.

CANNED GOODS   A few canned goods (without additives), such as tomato paste, water chestnuts, olives, tuna and sardines, are acceptable for emergencies. Choose canned tomato products without citric acid.

FROZEN VEGETABLES Stock some, such as frozen artichoke hearts or green peas, for soups and salads. Check labels and avoid those with sugar, vinegar and additives.

DELI SECTION Select corn tortillas and shun everything else. Check the label carefully to avoid preservatives and inspect package for mold.

CRACKERS If you can't find yeast- and sugar-free wholegrain crackers in the supermarket, look for them in the health food store.

CAUTION Don't overbuy! Purchase fresh foods frequently, as soon as possible after they are delivered to the store.

Health/Natural Food Stores

Although you can purchase most of your yeast-free foods at regular supermarkets, health/natural food stores are good sources of high-quality foods such as olive oil, raw butter and fertile eggs. It is as necessary to scrutinize labels in these stores as it is in supermarkets, for not all produce is organic, nor are all meats free from additives. Now that unsafe levels of EDB (ethylene dibromide), a carcinogenic fumigant, have been found in many foods (including high levels in grains and flours), choosing organic unfumigated grain is more important than ever.

Yeast-free crackers, breads and tortillas are commonly available at health/natural food stores. Select beans you have never tried before, such as azuki beans, or experiment with fresh herbs as well as specialty grains such as millet and brown rice. Be careful, however, of any packaged goods that claim to be "sugar free." Read label ingredients carefully, for usually the contents do include sweeteners. "Sugar free" is a misnomer, denoting only sucrose (table sugar). Most prepared and processed foods and many vitamin supplements contain yeast. Again, *read labels carefully*. It is best to make dressings and sauces from scratch and use fresh ingredients. Use the following brief checklists for your meal plans:

RECOMMENDED FOODS	FOODS TO BE AVOIDED
lean fresh meats, including beef and lamb	sugar in all forms, including honey and molasses

RECOMMENDED FOODS
all forms of fowl
organ meats
fresh game meat
deep sea fish

vegetables
greens
roots

complex starches in limited
quantities: legumes and grains

water:
  distilled
  mineral

fats and oils:
  olive oil
  butter

FOODS TO BE AVOIDED
dairy products, except butter
white flour products
seeds and nuts*

yeast- and mold-containing
foods (see pages 134–135):
vinegar, mushrooms, sauer-
kraut, cheeses

prepared sauces such as soy
sauce

juices

food additives, including citric acid

fruit

Planning: A Key Factor

One key to success in using these diets is to plan ahead. When
hunger strikes, it is all too easy to reach into the refrigerator
and grab the first thing available. Haphazard eating will not
assure balance and necessary nutrient intake. Plan your day to
include time for preparation of meals. This will help you adhere to your diet guidelines and speed the healing process.

Plan to keep one or two individual portions of a cooked
meat or soup in the freezer. Then you can select a package to
use at home or to take out with you, and allow it to defrost en
route.

Freezing Leftovers

Refrigerated food deteriorates in quality very rapidly. It also
supports the growth of bacteria and mold. To prevent this,
freeze all unused portions of meals that you wish to save each
day to use at a later date. Uncooked meat, poultry or seafood

*See page 9.

should be frozen until the day you plan to prepare it.* Small quantities of freshly cooked beans and grains are always best, but in emergencies larger quantities can be cooked and divided into individual portions to be frozen. An easy way to ensure quick defrosting is to freeze single portions in heavy plastic bags. Distribute the contents evenly. (Blocks of food take more time to defrost.)

If you are planning to be away from home all day, take along small snacks or a meal (see page 19) to avoid being caught hungry without your allowed foods.

*F. Granville Knight, M.D., author of *Physical Degeneration and Allergy*, and *What Are Pesticides Doing to Human Beings?*, in personal conversations repeatedly stated that freezing and thawing meats caused about a 20 percent loss of nutrients, which he felt was a good trade-off if one could obtain better-quality meats through frozen storage.

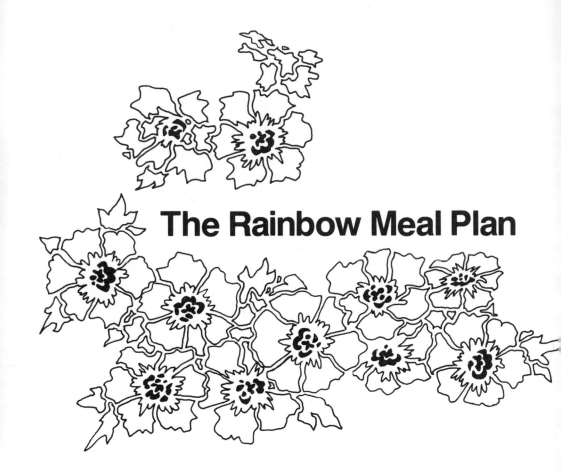

The Rainbow Meal Plan

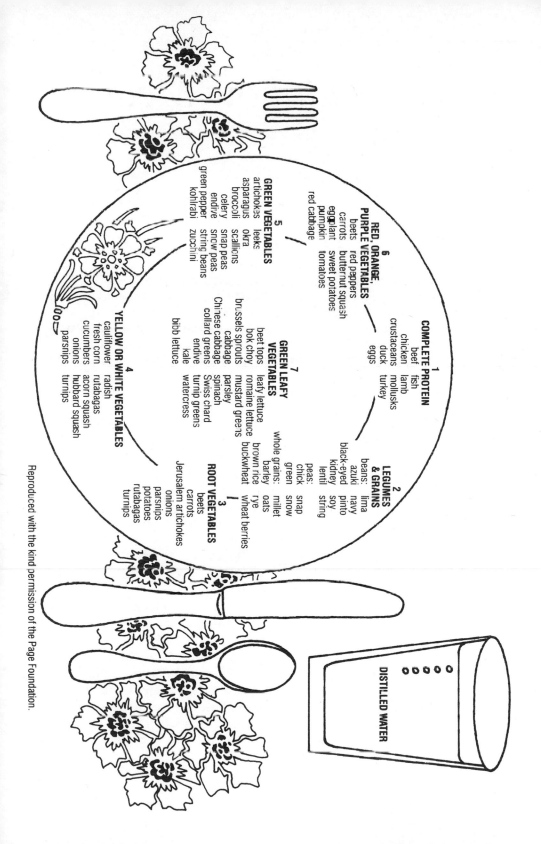

COMPLETE PROTEIN
beef
chicken
crustaceans
duck
eggs
fish
lamb
mollusks
turkey

**2
LEGUMES
& GRAINS**
beans:
azuki
black-eyed
kidney
lentil
peas:
chick
green
whole grains:
barley
brown rice
buckwheat
lima
navy
pinto
soy
string
snap
snow
millet
oats
rye
wheat berries

**3
ROOT VEGETABLES**
beets
carrots
Jerusalem artichokes
onions
parsnips
potatoes
rutabagas
turnips

**4
YELLOW OR WHITE VEGETABLES**
cauliflower
fresh corn
cucumbers
onions
parsnips
radish
rutabagas
acorn squash
hubbard squash
turnips

**5
GREEN VEGETABLES**
artichokes
asparagus
broccoli
celery
endive
green pepper
kohlrabi
leeks
okra
scallions
snap peas
snow peas
string beans
zucchini

**6
RED, ORANGE,
PURPLE VEGETABLES**
beets
carrots
eggplant
pumpkin
red cabbage
red peppers
butternut squash
sweet potatoes
tomatoes

**7
GREEN LEAFY
VEGETABLES**
beet tops
bok choy
brussels sprouts
cabbage
Chinese cabbage
collard greens
endive
kale
leafy lettuce
romaine lettuce
mustard greens
parsley
spinach
Swiss chard
turnip greens
watercress
bibb lettuce

DISTILLED WATER

The Rainbow Meal Plan

PRICE-PAGE-PACETTI DIET

Weston A. Price, D.D.S., a nutritional pioneer in the 1920s, observed eating patterns of healthy people throughout remote areas of the world. He attributed their optimal health to diets derived from indigenous whole foods, high in minerals, vitamins, dietary fiber, essential fatty acids, and an unidentified element he termed "Factor X." This mysterious factor was found to be a catalyst that enhances mineral absorption and assimilation. Price found it in environments as varied as the northern tundra and tropical rain forests. Price's work has been preserved in his classic text, *Nutrition and Physical Degeneration*, which includes photographic documentation of his findings.[4]

Dr. Melvin Page, also a dentist, was a colleague and protégé of Dr. Price. Having studied the Price research, he applied the findings to his patients. He advised them to avoid all refined foods, especially sugar. He found, through precise laboratory analyses, that when patients ate sugar and other refined foods, their blood chemistries became abnormal. When they followed a diet of fresh vegetables, whole grains and protein, their blood chemistries shifted toward normal.[5]

Homeostasis, the scientific word for internal balance, is the state of healthy blood chemistry observed by Dr. Page. In this steady, balanced state, humans can find health. In this state, the body maintains blood pressure, blood sugar, body temperature and other functions within a non-stressful range.

Homeostasis, the steady state of man, comes as part of our human heritage. We are equipped with systems, backup systems and emergency generators to maintain internal equilibrium.

Stress, from food, emotions, lack of rest, injury or nutritional deficiencies, can upset that equilibrium. The body can deal with occasional stress very efficiently. It's when stress becomes continuous that the body's balancing act is difficult, if not impossible, to maintain.

Dr. Page observed that stress from food was a powerful

insult to the body's equilibrium. Sugar was found to be the prime offender. Laboratory analyses showed that some Page patients experienced upset blood chemistry for four days after eating sugars. This included honey, molasses, and syrups. On the basis of these studies, Dr. Page recommended no refined sugars or even fruits during periods of recovery from illness. During times of health, he recommended only occasional desserts and fruit.

Another dentist and nutritionist, Bruce Pacetti, has made exciting contributions and additions to the work begun by Drs. Price and Page. Dr. Pacetti has observed that many patients with chronic health problems, especially candidiasis, have developed sensitivities or allergies to foods. Their digestive systems are not working efficiently. When foods are not digested completely, toxins are produced in the intestines and then absorbed into the bloodstream. Incomplete digestion also means that valuable nutrients are not being absorbed from foods. All this—toxins and lack of nutrients—contributes to tipping the internal balance to imbalance. Lack of homeostasis, our steady internal state, prevents healing. To allow for better digestion, reduce the allergic reaction to foods, and provide a wide range of essential vitamins, minerals and enzymes, Dr. Pacetti has developed the Rainbow Meal Plan. This beautiful, colorful array of vegetables, whole grains and protein offers a variety of textures, tastes and nutrients. Possible allergic reactions are minimized by eating only a small portion of each item. The effectiveness of the Rainbow Meal Plan for Candida patients is corroborated by Shirley S. Lorenzani, Ph.D., whose articles, lectures and tapes have inspired thousands of other Candida patients to modify their eating habits and once again enjoy good health.[6]

The Rainbow Plate includes small portions of seven food groups: complete protein; grain or legume; root vegetable; yellow or white vegetable; green vegetable; red, orange, or purple vegetable; and green leafy vegetable.

An extremely ill person with poorly functioning digestion will want to begin with very small portions, as small as an eighth of a cup of each item. Such a person may need to eat many small meals each day. Eating every two hours may be necessary until digestion improves.

Others may eat larger portions. There is no need to measure your portions meticulously. You may want to use a measuring cup or spoon at first, but soon you can estimate accurately.

It is easy to determine when your portion sizes have become too large. If you feel full after eating, you ate too much. The ideal Rainbow Plate will leave you feeling light and comfortable.

Why not begin by eating very small portions? If that works for you, continue until your body demands larger portions. Remember to keep all items approximately the same size. Have the same amount of green leafy vegetable as you do grains or beans.

Complete guidelines for the Rainbow Meal Plan are as follows:

1.   Prepare and eat small portions (these may range from an eighth to a quarter of a cup of *each* of the seven categories in the beginning).
2.   Choose one food from each category.
3.   All vegetables should be raw or gently steamed, not overcooked.
4.   Kelp powder, sea salt, plain pepper and raw butter can be used in moderation.
5.   Digestion begins in your mouth. Chew thoroughly and enjoy every bite.
6.   Drink only distilled water. Sip small amounts with meals and drink at least eight glasses a day between meals.
7.   Eat as many meals per day as desired. Use these meals for a snack; conform to these guidelines and space your meals at least two hours apart.
8.   To aid digestion, relax before, during and after your meals. Keep your thoughts and conversation calm.

This meal plan is satisfying in many ways. Once you have become familiar with shopping for a variety of foods, storing them conveniently, and cooking with a steamer, it will be easy and delightful. If variety is the spice of life, there is no question that it is the spice of eating! Taste buds will soon anticipate the many tastes and textures on the Rainbow Plate. Cells will appreciate the many vitamins, minerals and enzymes.

What to do when you eat out? Salad bars and lightly cooked vegetables and proteins provide a simple solution. Sharing an entree with a friend is often a way to economize for your health and finances. Protein portions in most restaurants are more than adequate for two people.

Can you take a Rainbow Meal to work? Certainly. Just prepare several meals at breakfast and pack one or two for your time away from home. Soups and stews containing foods from the seven groups are a delicious and simple way to eat on the job. A large thermos can provide several meals.

While many people experience the Rainbow Meal Plan as a satisfying, orderly, disciplined way of eating, others interpret it as too structured, too demanding. If you find yourself spending too much time planning and preparing for meals, shift to the Modified Food Plan featured in this book. The carbohydrate content of each recipe as well as the chart on pages 136–140 are tools for the reader taking a physician's advice to follow a diet low in carbohydrates. Dr. Crook notes that the amount for each person can vary as much as 100 grams daily, so be sure to consult your personal physician about your diet.[7] You may also choose to eat some of your meals from the Rainbow Plan and others from the Modified Plan. You might eat breakfast from the Modified Food Plan, and enjoy a Rainbow Plate for lunch and dinner. Both the Rainbow Plate and the Modified Food Plan are excellent styles of eating that can give you the dietary support necessary to regain abundant health.

Select equal portions from the following seven food categories:

COMPLETE PROTEIN

ONE

MEATS

beef	gelatin, plain	mutton
beef brains	*incomplete protein*	rabbit
beef heart	goat meat	sweetbreads
beef tongue	goose	veal
buffalo	kidney	wild
frog legs	lamb	*squirrel, deer*
	liver	

FOWL:

chicken
duck
goose
organ meats
  from chicken, turkey, etc.

pheasant
turkey

EGGS:

chicken
duck
goose

FISH, MOLLUSKS AND CRUSTACEANS

abalone
anchovy
bass
carp
caviar
clam
cod
crab
crappie
crayfish
fish roe
flounder

haddock
halibut
herring
lobster
mackerel
  Spanish
mullet
  Lisa
oysters
perch
pompano
red snapper

salmon
sardine
scallop
shark
shrimp
smelt
sole
sunfish
swordfish
tuna
whitefish
whiting

TWO

GRAINS:

amaranth
barley
buckwheat
corn
flaxseed

millet
oats
oat bran
psyllium seed husks

rice
  brown
sprouted grains
  barley, wheat, rye

LEGUMES

beans	*peas*	*lentils*
azuki	black-eyed	
black	chick garbanzos	
kidney	snap	
lima	split	
mung		
navy		
pinto		
soy		
string		

VEGETABLES

THREE

ROOT VEGETABLES:

anise root	onion	radish
beet	parsnip	rutabaga
carrot	parsley root	turnip
celeriac	Irish potato	yam
celery root	sweet potato	
Jerusalem		
artichokes		

FOUR

YELLOW AND WHITE VEGETABLES:

avocado	cucumber	rutabaga
bean sprouts, mung	endive, Belgian	squash
beans, wax	jicama	*yellow, crook-necked*
cauliflower	onion	turnip
corn	parsnip	
	radish	

FIVE

GREEN VEGETABLES

artichoke, globe
asparagus
bean, lima
beans, string
broccoli

celery
kohlrabi
leeks
okra
olive
pea pods
   edible
peas, green
peas, sugar snap

pepper, green
sprouts
scallions
zucchini

SIX

RED, ORANGE AND PURPLE VEGETABLES:

beets
carrots
eggplant
pumpkin
red cabbage

red bell peppers
sweet potato
tomato
winter squash
yam

SEVEN

LEAFY GREEN VEGETABLES

artichokes, globe
beet tops
bok choy
brussels sprouts
cabbage
chicory
chives
collards

dandelion
endive
escarole
kale
lettuce, iceberg
lettuce, red leaf
lettuce, romaine
mustard greens

parsley
spinach
summer savory
turnip greens
watercress
Swiss chard
sunflower greens

Typical Rainbow Recipes

A RAINBOW BREAKFAST

A Rainbow meal can be used for breakfast but if you feel like a more traditional meal, you might enjoy the egg combinations below.

Equipment needed:
Stainless steel pot: 2 or 3 quart size with lid
Stainless steel steamer basket
One custard cup
Cutting board with sharp knife

Complete protein:
Raw egg, in the shell

Starch:
¼ cup cooked brown rice

Root vegetable:
¼ cup raw shredded beets or carrots

White vegetable:
¼ cup onions, chopped

Green vegetable:
¼ cup celery, chopped

Red vegetable:
Medium tomato, finely chopped

Leafy green vegetable:
Parsley, coarsely chopped

CARBOHYDRATES	GRAMS
egg	**.50**
rice	**9.25**
beets or	**3.00**
carrots	**2.75**
onions	**3.75**
tomato	**7.10**
parsley	**1.20**
celery	**1.20**
	26.85
	(approximately)

Place steamer basket and ½ inch water in pot. Place whole egg in the steamer basket, cover the pot and bring water to boil. Reduce heat to medium and set timer for six minutes. Put cooked rice (in custard cup) in pot beside egg. (Re-cover the pot after each addition.) After two minutes, add beets or carrots and onions. After two additional minutes, add celery. After another two minutes, add tomato and parsley. Remove the egg from the pan when the timer says 6 to 7 minutes; hold the egg under running cold water briefly to stop the cooking process. Crack open the egg onto the plate, or into an egg cup. Dividing the plate into three areas, serve the beets or carrots onto the second area, the rice onto the third. Scoop the remaining vegetables over the egg and over the rice, as desired. Add a pat of butter and season. Serves one.

Note: In general, denser foods, such as meats and root vegetables, are added at the beginning of the cooking process, the more delicate foods later. If necessary, lift the lid from time to time and remove cooked vegetables that have reached a brilliant color, to avoid overcooking.

Note: The carbohydrate contents for all recipes are approximate and are based on analyses of the dishes as prepared; thus variations in carbohydrate values for the same amounts of the same ingredients will be noticed. This range of variation depends on seasonal changes in foods, differences among varieties and methods of preparation.

A ONE-POT RAINBOW MEAL

This is a step-by-step procedure for preparing a Rainbow meal. We have chosen a variety of colors to make it particularly attractive; however, you can make substitutions from the list of seven food categories. Adjust the cooking time, if necessary. *Remember: Always measure 1/4 cup of each ingredient, or the appropriate amount for the individual.* Chicken should be cooked thoroughly. Vegetables should be bright and crunchy.

Equipment needed:
Stainless steel pot: 2 or 3 quart size with lid
Stainless steel steamer basket
Pyrex custard cup
Cutting board with sharp knife

Complete protein:
One boned chicken thigh

Grain:
¼ cup cooked brown rice or millet

Root vegetable:
¼ cup raw carrot scrubbed clean, sliced

Red vegetable:
small wedge of red cabbage

Green vegetable:
¼ cup broccoli florets

White vegetable:
¼ cup cauliflower florets

Leafy green vegetable:
handful of spinach leaves

Seasonings:
butter or olive oil, sea salt or kelp

CARBOHYDRATES	GRAMS
rice	**9.25**
carrot	**4.2**
cauliflower	**1.5**
broccoli	**1.5**
cabbage	**1.75**
spinach	**1.5**
	19.7
	(approximately)

Place steamer basket and ½ cup of water in pot with lid. Bring water to boil and reduce to medium heat. Place chicken in steamer basket along with rice (in custard cup). Cover pot and steam for approximately ten to twelve minutes. After two minutes, add carrots and cabbage wedge. After four additional minutes, add broccoli and cauliflower. Check for doneness. Add spinach leaves for the final minute. Remove all items that are done and, if necessary, steam others such as the chicken a few moments longer. Serves one.

RAINBOW SOUP

Allow ¼ cup of each ingredient per person

Water, one cup

Complete protein:
lean beef cut into bite-size pieces

Root:
carrot, chopped fine

White:
onions, minced

Green:
celery, sliced

Red:
tomato, cut into bite-size pieces

Leafy green vegetable:
parsley, snipped

Legumes:
cooked lentils

Seasoning:
Olive oil

CARBOHYDRATES	GRAMS
lentils	**10.0**
carrots	**2.7**
onions	**3.4**
celery	**1.2**
tomato	**3.0**
parsley	**1.3**
per serving	**21.6**
(approximately)	

Heat water to boiling and reduce to low heat. Add beef, carrots and onions, stirring and cooking until softened. Add celery and continue to cook. Add tomato, lentils and finally parsley. Season as desired, and add ½ to 1 tablespoon of olive oil per person before serving.

This soup can be prepared in large quantity and frozen in individual serving-size containers. It makes an unusual but excellent Rainbow Breakfast.

RAINBOW SALAD BAR

This makes a beautiful party buffet. Set out an assortment of leafy greens, sliced or chopped vegetables, chilled beans and/or grains, and bite-size cubes of meat, using an individual serving bowl for each item. Prepare grated vegetables just before serving to avoid deterioration. Arrange several different items on a large tray and provide spoons or tongs for servings.

Here are some suggestions to stir your imagination:

Leafy greens, torn into bite-size pieces:
alfalfa sprouts
Chinese cabbage, slivered
lettuce leaves
spinach
watercress

Green vegetables:
bell pepper, sliced
broccoli, raw, in florets
celery, sliced
peas, steamed
snap peas, raw
zucchini, raw, sliced

Root vegetables:
beets, slivered or grated
carrots, slivered or grated
jicama, in cubes or strips
radishes, sliced

White vegetables:
cauliflower, in florets
corn, freshly picked and raw
cucumber, sliced or chopped

Red vegetables:
Red cabbage, shredded
red pepper (sweet), sliced or chopped
tomatoes, whole cherry
tomatoes, chopped

Beans, cooked and drained:
chickpeas
kidney beans
lentils

Grains, cooked, chilled and fluffed with a fork. They should be crumbly:
millet
rice

Meats or equivalent, cooked and cut into strips or cubes:
beef
chicken
sliced fish
hard-boiled eggs

Dressings:

Offer one or more of the dressings from this book (see pages 110–115), or have olive oil and lemon juice available with little bowls of freshly snipped parsley, chives and other herbs, salt and kelp in shakers. For non-Candida guests you may wish to add a basket of crackers or warm bread and butter, or a bowl of grated cheese. Just remember, these are *not* in the Candida diet.

The Modified Meal Plan

This meal plan is based on a variety of healthful recipes that exclude foods detrimental to the Candida patient. There are many other benefits bestowed by this healing diet, in addition to the control of Candida infection.

Freshness is the basis for the eating plan, which emphasizes elimination of food additives and mold-contaminated foods as well as fermented beverages and foods. You will discover that you will begin to lose the food addictions that once fed your Candida. You will acquire a new taste for healthful, freshly prepared meals.

The recipes selected combine the basic foods of your diet in new and interesting ways. Basic preparation techniques are given for meats, poultry, beans, grains and egg dishes that retain freshness but retard spoilage.

Candida patients must be especially careful in the selection, storage and preparation of foods in order to gain full nutritional benefit.

Seasoning for Nutrition and Pleasure

Using herbs and spices is a wonderful way to add flair to a simple meal. Also, many herbs and spices are reported to possess health-giving properties. These include allspice, cinnamon, clove, coriander, dill, garlic, onion, mustard, oregano, rosemary, summer savory and thyme. Select fresh varieties as much as possible, since dried herbs are mold-prone. The use of fresh herbs may become your trademark as a cook, and the kudos may stimulate you to start growing your own.[8]

You will want to start scissor-snipping your crop. To scissor-snip herbs in a cup, open and close the scissors repeatedly, cutting through the herbs until you have the small size desired. Some varieties may need to be purchased pre-packaged at the food stores. Check labels for any additions of sugar, yeast or additives that you need to avoid.

Use pasteurized butter only if certified raw butter is unavailable. The latter adds valuable nutrients as well as flavor to dishes. Olive oil, too, is nutritious and brings a distinct flavor and aroma to dishes. For a quick dressing, combine freshly-squeezed lemon juice with olive oil.[9] Keep a small quantity in the refrigerator and add scissor-snipped parsley, chives or mint. It will remain fresh for a few days and add zest to vegetables and salads.

Salt is included in the following recipes. You can choose to use it or not, a determination best made in consultation with your physician. If there is no medical problem, it will be your personal choice. Whole sea salt is preferable to refined salt. An unrefined salt containing trace minerals is also available.

RECIPES

*B*REAKFAST
*C*EREALS

PSYLLIUM SEED
BEVERAGE OR BREAKFAST

Beverage:

1 heaping teaspoon ground psyllium seed
water, 8-ounce glass

Pour ground psyllium seeds into glass and stir briskly. Drink at once as a bulk-forming supplement. Follow with another glass of water.

Breakfast:

2 heaping teaspoons ground psyllium seed
8 ounces broth, liquid from steamed vege-
tables, or herb tea

Stir psyllium seed into steaming or cold liquid and serve as cereal. Be sure to follow serving with 8 ounces of liquid.

CORN MEAL MUSH

1 cup boiling water
½ teaspoon kelp or dulse
¼ cup freshly ground undegerminated cornmeal

CARBOHYDRATES	GRAMS
corn meal	**27.0**
per serving	**13.5**

In top of double boiler, directly on burner, bring 1 cup of water to boil. Add kelp or dulse. Meanwhile, mix corn meal with ¼ cup cold water. Add this mixture to boiling water, stirring constantly and carefully. (It will bubble.) Continue to cook about 3 minutes. Then return top to double boiler bottom, cover, and continue steaming about 15 minutes, stirring often. Serve with butter. Serves two.

CREAM OF GRAIN CEREAL

2 tablespoons any whole grain below:
rice
wheat
oats
barley
rye
½ cup boiling water

CARBOHYDRATES	GRAMS
rice	**10.0**
wheat	**8.5**
barley	**19.0**
rye	**17.0**
oats	**11.5**

Grind grain in mini-mill. Stir into boiling water. Reduce heat, cover and simmer 5 minutes. Serve with thick cream, Fake Cream (see page 124) or butter. Serves one.

FLAXSEED CEREAL

½ cup boiling water
¼ cup flaxseed, freshly ground in mini-mill

Slowly stir flaxseed into boiling water. Mix well and cover pot. Remove from stove and allow to mellow on trivet for about 5 minutes. Serve with thick cream, Fake Cream (see p. 124) or butter. Serves one.

OAT BRAN CEREAL

⅓ cup oat bran[10]
1 cup boiling water

CARBOHYDRATES	GRAMS
per serving	**16**

Stir oat bran very slowly into the boiling water, stirring constantly. Return to boil. Reduce heat and cook until desired thickness, approximately 2 to 3 minutes, stirring often. Remove from heat and serve with melted butter. Serves one.

STEAMED WHOLEGRAIN CEREAL

⅓ cup wholegrain: wheat, oats, barley or rye
1 cup boiling water

CARBOHYDRATES	GRAMS
wheat	**11.3**
oats	**15.2**
barley	**25.3**
rye	**22.6**

The night before serving, bring 1 cup water to boil. Stir in grain. Return to boil and simmer 10 minutes. Cover and let sit overnight. Next morning bring mixture to simmer, adding more water if necessary. Continue heating until of desired consistency, about 5 minutes for oats, 10 for wheat or barley, and 15 to 30 minutes for rye. Serve with thick cream or butter. Serves two.

EGGS

Health/natural food stores sell good quality eggs produced by free-range chickens. Try them! The shells should be uniform in shape, smooth and dense, so you really have to tap sharply on the rim of the skillet in order to crack them. When the raw egg falls onto a plate or dish, it displays a well-rounded yolk of bright orange, surrounded by a clearly defined circle of egg white. You should be able to lift the yolk with your fingers and draw the white of the egg with it.[11]

Soft-Cooked Eggs

Use a small saucepan if you are cooking only one or two eggs. Place eggs in saucepan, cover with water. Heat water, using a medium setting, until it begins to boil. Turn heat off, cover pot and allow the eggs to sit for 5 minutes. Remove eggs from hot water. Rinse them under cold water to stop cooking process.

Hard-Cooked Eggs

Initially, plan to cook an extra egg that you can use to check for doneness. You will then have the experience for future reference. Submerge large eggs in sufficient water to cover them. Cook uncovered over medium heat until water bubbles begin to appear. Reduce heat, cover pot, and continue to simmer for 24 minutes. Do not overcook. Open your extra egg under cold water and check yolk for doneness. There should be a hint of bright yellow in the center. If it is cooked sufficiently, use a slotted spoon and immediately remove the remaining eggs from the pot and plunge them into a bowl of cold water. Allow them to remain for 5 minutes, return them to the hot water for 2 minutes and then remove them. You can now peel them effortlessly under cold water.

BASIC OMELET

2 eggs
2 tablespoons water
dash salt
seasonings as desired
1 tablespoon butter

CARBOHYDRATES	GRAMS
butter	.1
eggs	1.0
	1.1

Beat eggs. Add water, salt and seasonings and beat until blended. Melt butter in skillet over low heat. Pour in egg mixture, and as it cooks, push uncooked portion of egg mixture to outside edge, allowing uncooked egg to reach hot pan surface. Tilt pan as necessary. While top is still slightly moist, roll omelet or fold in half and slide onto plate. Serves one.

CURRIED VEGETABLE OMELET

2 tablespoons butter
¾ cup onions cut in slivers
2 slices ginger root
1 clove garlic cut in half
1 teaspoon curry powder
6 tablespoons turkey broth
1 tablespoon butter
3 or 4 eggs
2 tablespoons water
¾ cup bell pepper, cut in thin strips
1¼ cups bok choy leaves, cut into strips
½ cup snow peas
½ cup celery, cut diagonally in slices

CARBOHYDRATES	GRAMS
butter	.3
onions	12.0
curry	1.1
eggs (4)	2.0
bell pepper	2.9
bok choy	2.2
snow peas	5.0
celery	2.5
	28.0
per serving	14.0

Over low heat, melt butter in large skillet. Cut onions lengthwise in slivers. Sauté with ginger root and garlic until soft. Discard garlic and ginger. Add curry powder and broth and simmer. Meanwhile, melt butter over low heat in a second skillet. Beat eggs and water and pour into second skillet. Let cook a few minutes. Now add remaining vegetables to onion mixture, cover and simmer. When eggs are done, but still moist, fold into an omelet and serve on plate. Spoon vegetables over eggs. Serves two.

Variation: Spinach or other greens may be used in place of bok choy.

SPANISH OMELET

¼ cup water
¼ cup onions, chopped
¼ cup celery, chopped
¼ cup green pepper, chopped
¼ cup zucchini or crookneck squash, chopped
1 tablespoon arrowroot (optional)
2 tablespoons water
½ cup tomato, chopped
2 eggs
1 teaspoon butter
¼ cup parsley, scissor-snipped

CARBOHYDRATES	GRAMS
onions	**4.0**
celery	**1.3**
green pepper	**1.0**
zucchini	**1.4**
arrowroot	**7.0**
tomato	**5.0**
eggs	**1.0**
butter	**.1**
parsley	**1.2**
	22.0

Begin cooking onions in water in vapor seal pot* over medium heat, reducing heat to low when water begins to boil.[12] Add celery, green pepper and squash and continue cooking until soft. Do not overcook. Meanwhile, stir arrowroot into water, mixing well. Move vegetables to edge of pan and stir arrowroot mixture into cooking water. Add tomatoes, reduce heat to simmer and cover. Beat eggs. Melt butter in skillet over low heat. Pour eggs into pan and allow to cook gently. When done, fold omelet, remove from pan. Spoon sauce over omelet. Sprinkle parsley over all, and serve. Serves one.

*If vapor seal is unavailable, increase water.

SPICED EGGS

The sweet flavor of the nutmeg blends nicely with that of the onions in this recipe.

¼ cup water
¼ cup onions, sliced
½ cup summer squash, chopped
½ cup each spinach, bok choy and watercress, torn into small pieces
1 or 2 eggs
⅛ teaspoon nutmeg
1 to 2 teaspoons butter
¼ cup tomato, sliced

CARBOHYDRATES	GRAMS
onions	**4.0**
squash	**2.8**
spinach	**1.0**
eggs (2)	**1.0**
butter	**.1**
tomato	**2.5**
	11.4

Cook onions in a vapor seal pot over low heat.* As onions begin to soften, add squash. Cook 4 or 5 minutes. Add leafy greens and cook until soft. Do not overcook. Spoon vegetables into a bowl, reserving cooking water. Beat eggs and add nutmeg and 2 tablespoons cooking water. Melt butter over low heat and pour eggs into pan. Let cook a few minutes. While top is still moist, fill with vegetables. When eggs are done, fold into an omelet and serve on a plate. Serves one.

*Increase water if vapor seal pot is not used.

Appetizers

TORTILLA CHIPS

If you wish to slip a few tortilla chips into a bowl of vegetables, try this recipe. Mix the chips with raw carrots, celery, bell peppers, cucumbers, broccoli, cauliflower, turnips, jicama, Jerusalem artichokes, zucchini or cooked globe artichoke leaves.

corn tortillas 5″ size, commercial

CARBOHYDRATES	GRAMS
8 chips	**5.0**

Preheat oven to 400°F. Cut tortilla into 8 pieces. Place on a cookie sheet and bake 6 minutes. Turn and bake 3 more minutes.

Note: Candida patients should limit themselves to not more than 6 chips, and should not use chips with bean dips. Instead try the avocado, tuna, eggplant or deviled egg dips. Also, omit beans and grains from the next meal.

CHICKEN LIVER PATE

2 tablespoons chicken fat
¼ cup onions minced
1 clove garlic, minced
1½ cups chicken livers*
½ cup chicken broth (concentrated)
pinch of ground allspice, mace and thyme

CARBOHYDRATES	GRAMS
onions	**3.0**
garlic	**.5**
livers	**15.0**
	18.5
¼ cup serving	**4.5**

*Chicken livers should be from biologically-raised poultry; otherwise, they may have a residue of arsenicals or cadmium. If such poultry is unavailable use calf's or lamb liver.

Rinse chicken livers and drain on paper towel. Chop coarsely and set aside. Cook onions and garlic in chicken fat over low heat until onions are soft. Add livers. Cook over a low heat for another minute or so, stirring occasionally. Add chicken broth, stir, cover and simmer 7 or 8 minutes longer or until livers are firm and no longer pink. Puree in a blender or mash well with potato masher or fork. Add spices and blend. Chill 2 to 3 hours. Mixture will thicken. Serve as a dip for raw vegetables. Makes about 1 cup.

LIVER PATE

Leftover broiled lamb or calf's liver (about ½ pound)
Homemade Mayonnaise (see page 114)
herbed salt
1 clove of garlic, pressed
1 hard-boiled egg
chopped celery, parsley and/or other vegetables (about 1 cup)

CARBOHYDRATES	GRAMS
liver ½ lb.	**9.0**
garlic	**.5**
egg	**.5**
mayonnaise, ¼ cup	**.6**
vegetables	**6.0**
	16.6

Grind any amount of leftover liver in meat grinder or blender. Add Homemade Mayonnaise, salt, garlic, egg and vegetables. Serve with yeast-free crackers or raw vegetables. Makes about 2 cups.

SALMON PATE

2 cups fresh cooked salmon, drained
⅓ cup Homemade Mayonnaise (see page 114)
3 artichoke hearts, steamed and mashed
1 green onion, chopped
3 tablespoons fresh or 1 teaspoon dried dillweed
¼ teaspoon mustard powder
1 tablespoon lemon juice

CARBOHYDRATES	GRAMS
salmon	**0.0**
artichoke	**2.5**
onion	**.8**
mayonnaise	**.8**
lemon	**1.0**
	5.1

Remove skin and bones from salmon, and puree in a blender or mash well with a fork. Add remaining ingredients and blend. Chill for 2 to 3 hours. Garnish with cucumber slices and serve with raw vegetables and yeast-free crackers. 2 cups.

TONGUE PATE

1 pound beef or calf's tongue, cooked
2 tablespoons butter
2 shallots, 4 or 5 scallions or 2 tablespoons onions, minced
½ cup celery
2 tablespoons cooking broth from tongue
1 stick soft butter
½ teaspoon scissor-snipped basil
1 teaspoon scissor-snipped oregano
1 teaspoon lemon juice
½ cup scissor-snipped parsley
seasoning salt to taste

CARBOHYDRATES	GRAMS
tongue	**2.0**
butter	**0.2**
scallions	**3.2**
celery	**2.3**
butter	**.8**
parsley	**2.5**
lemon	**.4**
	11.4

Skin and trim cooked tongue and blend or finely grind it. Sauté vegetables in butter, broth and herbs. Mix ground mixture, soft butter and parsley. Mold or shape into pâté and chill one hour. Serve with raw vegetables. Freeze any leftover pâté. Makes about 2 cups.

DEVILED EGG DIP

4 hard-cooked eggs, shelled (see page 34)
4 tablespoons Homemade Mayonnaise (see
   page 114)
⅛ teaspoon nutmeg or to taste (optional)
½ teaspoon mustard powder (optional)

CARBOHYDRATES	GRAMS
eggs	2.0
mayonnaise	.7
herbs	1.0
	3.7

Blend all ingredients. Chill. Serve with raw vegetables. Makes
1 cup.

Variation: Season to taste with other herbs such as curry powder, tarragon, or basil.

EGGPLANT CAVIAR

This mixture, also known as Poor Man's Caviar, can be used as
a dip with raw vegetables or to stuff celery.

1½ cups onions, diced
2 cloves garlic, minced
2 tablespoons butter
1 medium eggplant, chopped
⅓ cup water
¼ cup olive oil
¼ cup lemon juice
2 tablespoons fresh basil, minced, or
   1 teaspoon dried basil
2 tablespoons sesame seeds (optional)

CARBOHYDRATES	GRAMS
onions	21.0
garlic	1.0
butter	.2
eggplant	18.0
lemon	4.8
sesame seeds	3.3
	48.3
per ¼ cup	6.0

Soften onion and garlic in butter over low heat. Add eggplant
and water. Cover pot and cook over medium heat for 2 minutes. Reduce heat and simmer 10 minutes. Stir in remaining
ingredients. Puree in 2 batches in blender. Chill. Makes approximately 2 cups.

GARBANZO DIP

2 cups garbanzo beans, cooked, drained (save liquid)
¼ to ½ cup green onions, chopped
2 cloves garlic, minced
2 tablespoons lemon juice
½ cup olive oil
2 cups parsley, chopped
½ teaspoon dried or 1 tablespoon fresh basil
¼ cup sesame seeds (optional)

CARBOHYDRATES	GRAMS
garbanzo beans	**122.0**
green onions ½ cup	**4.0**
garlic	**1.8**
lemon juice	**2.4**
olive oil	**trace**
parsley	**10.2**
herbs	**.4**
sesame seeds	**5.3**
1½ cups	**146.1**

Puree all ingredients in blender at low speed. If mixture is too thick, add a little cooking water from beans. Chill. Serve with raw vegetables. Makes 1½ cups.

Note: This dip, very high in carbohydrates, should be consumed in limited amounts.

GUACAMOLE DIP

1 cup avocado (1 large)
¼ cup onions, grated or finely chopped
¼ to ½ cup tomato, chopped fine
1 tablespoon lemon juice
1 clove garlic, minced (optional)
¼ cup finely chopped fresh cilantro leaves
salt and/or kelp to taste

CARBOHYDRATES	GRAMS
avocado	**15.0**
onions	**3.8**
tomato ½ cup	**5.0**
lemon juice	**1.2**
garlic	**.9**
cilantro	**.5**
per cup	**26.4**

Puree all ingredients in electric blender or mash avocado with a fork and mix in other ingredients. Chill. Serve with fresh raw vegetables. Makes 1 cup.

Variation: Substitute sweet basil or other favorite herbs if cilantro is unavailable.

MEXICAN BEAN DIP

1 cup pinto beans, cooked
1 cup tomato, chopped fine
¼ cup (or less) olive oil
½ teaspoon chili powder
½ teaspoon cumin
salt and/or kelp to taste

CARBOHYDRATES	GRAMS
pinto beans	**60.5**
tomato	**10.0**
olive oil	**trace**
seasoning	**1.0**
per cup	**71.5**
Variations: kidney beans	
total	**53.0**

Puree beans in a ricer (Foley mill) or mash with a fork. Add rest of ingredients and continue to rice or mash. Serve with vegetable as a dip. Makes about 1 cup.

Note: Candida patients need to limit themselves to a few tablespoons and omit beans and grain at the subsequent meal. This dip can be frozen in small portions and carried along with vegetables (cucumber, celery and jicama strips, etc.) in a box lunch.

Variations: Add 1 clove garlic, ¼ cup finely minced onion and some finely minced chili peppers. Substitute kidney beans for pinto beans.

MOCK TUNA DIP

This dip may be used to stuff celery or as a dip for fresh raw vegetables.

1 cup fish*, cooked and cooled
1 cup celery, chopped fine
1 cup parsley, minced
½ cup green onion, minced
¼ cup bell pepper, minced
¼ cup Homemade Mayonnaise (see page 114)
½ teaspoon dried or 1 tablespoon fresh tarragon, snipped
½ teaspoon dried or 1 tablespoon fresh dill weed

CARBOHYDRATES	GRAMS
fish	0.0
celery	4.0
parsley	5.0
green onion	3.0
mayonnaise	.7
pepper	2.4
herbs	1.0
	16.1

Mash fish and mix with chopped vegetables, mayonnaise and herbs.

*Substitute canned tuna if fresh fish is unavailable. Makes 2 cups.

SPLIT PEA-CURRY DIP

½ cup dried split peas
1½ cups water
2 tablespoons butter
2 tablespoons onions, chopped
½ cup carrot, sliced
¾ teaspoon curry powder

CARBOHYDRATES	GRAMS
cooked split peas	42.0
butter	.2
onions	2.0
carrot	5.5
curry powder	.9
per cup	50.6

Cook peas until well done, about 1½ hours. If necessary, add more water to prevent burning. Allow excess water to cook off.

Cool. (Peas should be the consistency of applesauce.) Sauté onions and carrots in butter over low heat. Stir into split peas. Add curry powder. Blend mixture until carrots are well mashed. Mixture will thicken as it cools. Serve as a dip for raw vegetables. Makes about 1 cup.

Soups

ASPARAGUS SOUP

1½ cups asparagus stalks
1 cup concentrated chicken broth
2 tablespoons butter
¼ cup shallots (or onions), chopped
1 cup celery, chopped
½ cup summer squash, sliced
1½ cups parsley, chopped
½ teaspoon dried or 1 tablespoon fresh basil

CARBOHYDRATES	GRAMS
asparagus	7.5
butter	.2
shallots	6.8
celery	4.7
squash	2.8
parsley	7.5
herbs	.4
	29.9
per serving	14.9

Chop asparagus stalks into 1-inch pieces. Simmer the tough stems in chicken broth for 20 to 30 minutes. In another pan melt butter over low heat, and add tender asparagus stems, shallots, celery and summer squash. Sauté until barely soft. Do not overcook. Add parsley and basil to mixture. Discard tough asparagus stems and add chicken broth to mixture. Pour into blender and blend for about a minute. Serves two.

AVOCADO-ASPARAGUS SOUP

1 pound asparagus, chopped
1 cup water
¼ cup onions, chopped
¼ teaspoon salt, optional
1 avocado, cut in chunks
2 eggs

CARBOHYDRATES	GRAMS
asparagus	10.0
onions	4.0
avocado	12.6
eggs	1.0
	27.6
per serving	13.8

Simmer asparagus lightly in 1 cup water until just tender. Pour with water into blender, add onion and salt, and puree at low speed. Add avocado and eggs and blend until smooth. Add broth or water to thin if needed. Serve hot or chilled. Serves two.

FRESH AVOCADO-TOMATO SOUP

You can serve this soup warm or chilled.

4 large tomatoes
1 medium avocado
2 green onions
¼ teaspoon ground dill seed
dash cayenne
1 cup chicken broth
1 teaspoon kelp
seasoning salt to taste
1 cup parsley, minced
1 cup celery, diced fine
1 tomato, chopped fine

CARBOHYDRATES	GRAMS
tomato	**40.0**
avocado	**12.6**
green onions	**2.0**
parsley	**5.1**
celery	**5.0**
tomato	**10.0**
seasonings	**2.0**
	76.7
1 of four servings	**19.2**
1 of three servings	**25.6**

Puree all ingredients except last three in blender at low speed. Stir soup mixture into remaining vegetables and warm over low heat, if desired. Or serve cold. Serves three to four.

HOT BORSCHT

½ cup raw potato with skins, diced fine
½ cup onions, diced
1 cup beets, diced
2 cups cabbage, slivered (Chinese cabbage is acceptable)
¼ cup butter
¾ cup chicken broth
2 tablespoons lemon juice
2 tablespoons parsley or chives, scissor-snipped

CARBOHYDRATES	GRAMS
potato	**12.9**
onions	**7.5**
beets	**13.4**
cabbage	**8.0**
butter	**.4**
lemon juice	**2.5**
parsley	**.6**
	45.3
per serving	**22.6**

Cook potato over low heat in a small amount of water until soft. Meanwhile, cook remaining vegetables over low heat in butter with a small amount of water until soft. When potatoes are cooked, add chicken broth and simmer until warmed. Puree this mixture at low speed in blender. Add potato puree and lemon juice to vegetable mixture, reheat, and serve. Garnish with snipped herbs. Serves two.

Note: Candida patients should limit themselves to one serving of this soup and omit beans and grains from the same meal.

CHICKEN SOUP

1 chicken, cut up
2 quarts water or broth
4 cloves of garlic, sliced (optional, to taste)
2 cups each of sliced celery, carrots,
    onions, peas
½ cup cooked brown rice
½ cup chopped parsley
herbs and seasoning to taste

CARBOHYDRATES	GRAMS
chicken	0.0
carrots	22.0
celery	9.4
peas	38.0
garlic	3.6
rice	18.5
parsley	2.5
onions	30.0
	124.0
per serving	12.4

Simmer chicken in water or stock for 40 minutes. Add vegetables and rice and simmer for 20 additional minutes. Serve broth and vegetables with chicken meat and top with scissor-snipped fresh parsley. Add herbs according to taste. Serves ten.

Note: Freeze surplus soup in portion-size containers. It is useful to have on hand some frozen portions of clear broth.

Variation: ¼ cup raw rice may be added to the water and simmered with the chicken.

CHICKEN SOUP II

3 pounds chicken backs, necks and wings
3 quarts water
3 carrots, sliced
4 stalks celery, sliced
4 cloves garlic, chopped
½ bunch parsley, chopped
4 green onions or 1 medium onion, chopped
1 teaspoon dried thyme (optional)

CARBOHYDRATES	GRAMS
chicken	0.0
carrots	7.0
celery	5.0
garlic	2.0
parsley	1.0
onions	4.0
	19.0
per 1 cup serving	1.5

Bring chicken and water to boil. Reduce heat, and simmer, covered, for 1 hour. Add vegetables and thyme and simmer 15 additional minutes or until tender. Makes 12 cups.

Note: Freeze surplus soup.

MEXICAN CHICKEN SOUP

1 quart chicken broth
1 cup onions, chopped
1 cup celery, chopped
1½ cups cooked chicken, slivered
¾ cup brown rice, cooked
1 cup cabbage, finely shredded
1 cup tomatoes, diced
¼ cup radishes
¼ cup scallions, chopped
1 cup parsley, chopped
½ cup green pepper, chopped
¾ cup avocado cubes (optional)
½ cup fresh cilantro leaves
salt and/or kelp to taste

CARBOHYDRATES	GRAMS
onions	**13.7**
celery	**4.7**
rice	**28.6**
cabbage	**6.0**
tomatoes	**10.3**
radishes	**2.0**
scallions	**1.6**
parsley	**5.0**
green pepper	**2.5**
avocado	**9.2**
cilantro	**1.0**
	84.6
1 of 3 servings	**28.2**
1 of 4 servings	**21.1**

Bring chicken broth to a boil and reduce heat to simmer. Add onions and celery, and simmer a few minutes; add chicken and rice. As broth simmers, add remaining ingredients and continue stirring and simmering for 3 to 4 minutes longer, until vegetables are piping hot but still crunchy. Serves three to four.

Variations: If cilantro is unavailable, substitute ½ teaspoon thyme or 1 tablespoon fresh thyme. You can place the raw vegetables on a platter and invite guests to transfer their choices to individual soup bowls. Then ladle the hot broth over the raw vegetables for a steaming and crunchy soup.

EGG DROP SOUP

2 cups chicken broth
1 scallion, sliced
1 egg

CARBOHYDRATES	GRAMS
broth	**0.0**
scallion	**2.0**
egg	**.5**
	2.5
per serving	**1.3**

Warm scallion gently in broth. Beat egg and dribble it into hot soup while stirring rapidly so that egg coagulates into thin noodlelike strands. Continue to stir and cook only until egg is firm. Serves two.

GARDEN SOUP

A light soup, good any time. The colorful vegetables nourish the soul as well as the body.

1½ cups water
¼ cup purple-topped turnip, chopped
½ cup green beans, chopped
½ cup carrots, sliced
½ cup zucchini or summer squash, sliced
½ cup Chinese cabbage, shredded
1½ cups parsley, chopped
½ cup tomato, chopped
a generous pinch of thyme, rosemary, marjoram, dash seasoning salt (optional)

CARBOHYDRATES	GRAMS
turnip	**2.0**
green beans	**4.0**
carrots	**5.5**
squash	**3.5**
cabbage	**1.2**
parsley	**7.7**
tomato	**5.0**
	28.9
per serving	**14.4**

Bring water to a boil. Add turnip, beans and carrots. Simmer 3 to 5 minutes. Meanwhile, prepare zucchini and cabbage, and add them to pot. Continue to simmer a few more minutes.

Chop parsley and tomato, add and continue to simmer 2 more minutes. Crumble herbs and add them to pot. Add salt. Remove from heat and let sit a minute. Serves two generously.

GAZPACHO

2 cups tomatoes
¾ cup cucumber
¼ cup green pepper
¾ cup celery with leaves
¼ cup parsley
¼ cup scallions
1 clove garlic
¼ cup lemon or lime juice
1 to 2 tablespoons olive oil
½ teaspoon dried or 1 tablespoon fresh basil
¼ cup chicken broth and/or ¾ cup processed tomato juice (without additives)

CARBOHYDRATES	GRAMS
tomatoes	20.0
cucumber	4.0
green pepper	1.0
celery	.7
parsley	1.3
scallions	2.0
garlic	.9
lemon juice	4.8
olive oil	0.0
herbs	.5
tomato juice	8.0
	43.2
1 of 4 servings	10.8
1 of 3 servings	14.4

Chop vegetables and put half in blender along with garlic, lemon or lime juice, olive oil, basil, broth and tomato juice. Puree briefly. Turn into large bowl. Chop remaining vegetables very fine and stir them into blender mixture. Chill and serve. Serves three to four.

Variation: Substitute other herbs, chilies, or chili powder for basil. For a different flavor, stir in ¾ cup steamed, chilled, cubed fish, and ¾ cup cooked, chilled rice. Add more herbs, if desired.

HEARTY LENTIL SOUP

½ cup lentils
2 cups water
1 onion, chopped
3 stalks celery, chopped
1 carrot, chopped
3 tomatoes, chopped
1 clove garlic, minced
½ cup parsley, chopped
2 tablespoons tomato paste
2 tablespoons fresh or 1 teaspoon dried thyme
salt to taste
2 tablespoons olive oil

CARBOHYDRATES	GRAMS
lentils	**40.0**
onion	**15.0**
celery	**6.0**
carrot	**7.0**
tomato	**22.0**
garlic	**.9**
parsley	**2.6**
tomato paste	**6.0**
herbs	**1.0**
olive oil	**0.0**
	100.5
per serving	**25.1**

Bring lentils to a boil, reduce heat and simmer for about 1 hour. (If you are using sprouted lentils, heat water only to a near boil, reduce heat and simmer lentils 5–10 minutes.) Add chopped onions, celery and carrots and stir while simmering 10 additional minutes. Add chopped tomatoes and minced garlic and simmer 3 more minutes. Add chopped parsley, tomato paste, thyme and salt if desired. Simmer 3 more minutes. Stir in olive oil and serve. (Consistency may be thick. Add water if you desire to thin it.) Serves four.

Variations: This recipe, adapted from a conventional one, has less starch (lentils and carrots) and more non-starchy vegetables (onion and celery). To reduce the carbohydrate content, use fewer lentils and omit the tomato paste. Serve this soup with a green salad or leafy green vegetables for balance of vegetables. The Candida patient should limit this soup to one serving.

MARROW SOUP

Have your butcher split or slice shank or knuckle bones with an electric saw. Short ribs, oxtail, lamb trimmings or other inexpensive cuts of boned meat are good, too. Reserve the bones.

CARBOHYDRATES GRAMS
no carbohydrates.

Allow 2 cups of water for every cup of lean meat and bone. Cover the bones with pure cold water and let stand 1 hour. Heat gently to 175°F, and cook for 12 hours or until meat falls off the bone. Cool uncovered, and then remove the bones. Refrigerate. Do not skim off the fat until ready to reheat.

To use:
Gently simmer the meat and any fresh vegetables briefly in some of the broth, until the vegetables are tender. Freeze surplus marrow soup in single portion-size containers.

MINESTRONE SOUP

A colorful winter warmer-upper.

¾ cup cooked beans (white, kidney, or limas or fresh peas)
2 tablespoons butter
½ cup onions, chopped
1 clove garlic, minced
3 cups broth
1 cup carrots, sliced
½ cup green beans, chopped
½ cup zucchini, cut in half lengthwise and then sliced
¾ cup celery tops, sliced
2 cups green cabbage or Swiss chard, slivered
½ teaspoon dried oregano
½ teaspoon dried thyme
1 cup parsley, chopped
1 cup tomato, chopped
½ teaspoon salt or kelp
2 tablespoons olive oil (optional)

CARBOHYDRATES	GRAMS
beans	**30.0**
butter	**.2**
onions	**7.0**
garlic	**.5**
carrots	**16.7**
green beans	**4.0**
zucchini	**4.0**
celery	**3.0**
cabbage	**12.0**
parsley	**5.0**
tomato	**12.0**
herbs, oil	**0.0**
	94.4
per serving	**23.6**

Cook beans (see page 62) and set aside. Sauté onions and garlic in butter until soft. Add broth and bring to a boil over medium heat. Add carrots and green beans. Reduce heat and simmer 2 or 3 minutes. Add zucchini and celery and simmer until zucchini begins to soften. Add cabbage and herbs and simmer until cabbage begins to soften. Add beans and allow to warm. Add parsley, tomato and salt and let simmer another two minutes. Add olive oil and serve. Serves four.

Variation: Add beef, lamb, turkey or chicken to this soup to make a complete meal. In this case, the broth should match the flavor of the chosen meat.

SOUP SALAD

We hear that this soup was prescribed by a nutritionally-oriented doctor who encouraged his patients to drink it daily.

½ cup water or seasoned broth
1 zucchini with skin, chopped
2 stalks celery with leaves, chopped
½ onion, chopped
6 string beans, finely chopped
½ cup parsley, chopped
1 clove garlic, minced
1 bay leaf
½ teaspoon dried basil
2 tablespoons lemon juice
salt and/or kelp

CARBOHYDRATES	GRAMS
zucchini	2.5
celery	4.0
onion	7.5
string beans	3.5
parsley	2.5
garlic	.9
herbs	.5
lemon juice	2.4
	23.8
per serving	11.9

Bring water to a boil, and add vegetables and bay leaf. Reduce heat, cover and simmer 8 to 10 minutes. Stir in remaining ingredients and cool a few minutes. Remove bay leaf and puree soup in blender. Serves two.

TOMATO-EGGPLANT SOUP

This soup can be served warm or chilled.

¾ cup onions, diced
1 clove garlic, minced
1 tablespoon butter
½ medium eggplant, chopped
3 tablespoons water
1 cup parsley, chopped
1½ cups tomato, chopped
1 tablespoon fresh basil, minced or
　½ teaspoon dried basil
1½ tablespoon olive oil, or to taste
2 tablespoon lemon juice

CARBOHYDRATES	GRAMS
onions	12.0
garlic	.9
butter	.1
eggplant	9.2
tomato	15.0
parsley	5.1
herbs	.4
oil	0.0
lemon juice	2.4
	45.1
per serving	22.5

Soften onion and garlic in butter by cooking over low heat. Add eggplant and water, cover pot and simmer 10 minutes. Blend parsley, tomato, basil, oil and lemon juice in blender. Add the cooked mixture, puree and serve. Serves two.

TOMATO-WATERCRESS SOUP

1 tablespoon chicken fat or butter
½ cup leeks, chopped fine
1 garlic clove, minced
1½ cups chicken broth
½ cup potato, cubed
1½ cups tomato, chopped
2 cups watercress leaves, chopped
½ cup parsley, minced

CARBOHYDRATES	GRAMS
butter	.1
leeks	5.5
garlic	.5
potato	12.5
tomato	15.0
watercress	4.4
parsley	2.5
	40.0
per serving	20.0

Spoon fat into saucepan, add leeks and garlic, and cook covered over low heat for 6 to 8 minutes until tender. Stir occasionally. Add broth and potato. Bring to a boil over medium heat, then reduce heat and simmer until potato is tender, 10 to 15 minutes. Add tomato, watercress and parsley, and simmer 1 to 2 minutes. Cool to room temperature or chill. Serves two.

Variations: Substitute zucchini for potato and cook 5 minutes in broth. Substitute onion or scallion for leeks. Substitute cucumber for potato, and add with tomato rather than cooking it.

QUICK VEGETABLE-BEEF SOUP

Use a chuck roast, cutting meat into bite-size pieces and refrigerating while you simmer the bones with:

2 cups water
2 cups sliced carrots
2 cups sliced onions
2 cups chopped celery
2 cups green beans, cut in pieces
2 cups chopped cabbage
2 cups chopped fresh tomatoes
salt
fresh herbs to taste

CARBOHYDRATES	GRAMS
carrots	**22.0**
celery	**9.4**
green beans	**16.0**
cabbage	**12.0**
onions	**20.0**
tomatoes	**20.0**
six cups	**99.4**
per serving	**16.5**

Simmer the first five ingredients, covered, for 20 minutes. Then add the cabbage and meat. Simmer 10 minutes and remove bones. Simmer until meat is tender and then add the chopped fresh tomatoes, seasoned to taste with fresh herbs and sea salt. Simmer 5 minutes. If you can find canned tomatoes or tomato puree without additives and no citric acid, it makes a delightful flavor variation. Be sure to make enough extra to freeze in 1- or 2-cup packages so that it will be ready to thaw and heat when you are famished and need a quick meal. Serves six.

VICHYSSOISE

A cold soup for hot weather.

½ cup raw potato, finely diced
¾ cup leeks, sliced thin
¼ cup onions, diced
½ cup celery, diced small
1 tablespoon butter
½ cup chicken broth (or more, if desired)
½ cup cucumber, chopped fine
½ cup parsley, chopped
½ cup watercress, chopped
1 teaspoon lemon juice, optional
⅛ teaspoon ground mace

CARBOHYDRATES	GRAMS
potato	**12.9**
leeks	**8.2**
onions	**3.5**
celery	**2.5**
butter	**.1**
cucumber	**1.8**
parsley	**2.6**
watercress	**.5**
lemon juice	**.4**
	32.5
per serving	**16.3**

Cook potato in a small amount of water over low heat until soft, and set aside. Sauté leeks, onions and celery in butter over low heat for a few minutes. Add chicken broth and cook for 10 minutes or until vegetables are soft but not overcooked. Add remaining ingredients to soup. Pour potatoes and their cooking water into blender, add ¾ of soup mixture and purée at low speed. Pour mixture back into soup pan, stir in remaining ¼ of soup and chill. Serves two.

Note: Candida patients must limit themselves to 1 serving.

QUICK ZUCCHINI SOUP

2 cups unpeeled zucchini, coarsely chopped
¼ cup onions, chopped fine
1 cup chicken broth
2 tablespoons butter (optional)
1 cup parsley, chopped
⅛ teaspoon nutmeg

CARBOHYDRATES	GRAMS
zucchini	**11.0**
onions	**4.0**
parsley	**5.1**
butter	**.2**
herbs	**.3**
	20.6
per serving	**10.3**

Cook zucchini and onions in chicken broth over low heat until tender. Add butter, parsley and nutmeg. Let soup cool 2 or 3 minutes, then puree in blender on low speed. Serves two.

LEGUMES AND GRAINS

Adelle Davis suggests that you pre-soak dried beans for several hours and then freeze them in the soaking liquid, so that cooking time can be cut in half.[13] Simply soak beans for 2 hours in water to cover. Freeze 2 hours, and then cook in a cup of broth or steamer water.

Although peanuts are a member of the legume family, they should be avoided when on a healing diet.[14]

If possible, grind your own grains and use at once. Try to use them sparingly because they are high in carbohydrates. For this reason, use only small amounts of yeast-free breads and crackers and tortillas. Avoid packaged breakfast cereals.

Add cooked grains to soups or salads as crouton substitutes. They soak up the tangy flavor of salad dressing. Store grains in containers with tight-fitting covers to prevent moisture and insect infestation. Place in a cool, dry area to retard rancidity.

BASIC BEAN RECIPE

1 cup dried beans (except lentils or split peas)
1 or 2 bay leaves (helps digestion)
3 cups water

CARBOHYDRATES GRAMS
Most beans are about **40** grams per cup cooked or **10** grams per ¼ cup portion.

Soak beans in cold water for 6 to 8 hours (in refrigerator if kitchen is warm). Remove any beans that float. Bring beans to a boil and simmer for 1½ to 2½ hours or until tender. Do not add salt until tender. Remove bay leaves.

Quick soak method:
Bring water to a boil. Add beans slowly so boiling does not stop. Remove pot from heat and let stand covered, 1 hour. Cook beans as directed above.

Note: Garbanzo beans require more cooking water and cooking time. Use 4 cups of water and cook for 3 hours. Soybeans require 3 hours or more. Lentils and split peas may be cooked, unsoaked, in 3 cups water, for 45 to 60 minutes, or until tender.

BASIC BROWN RICE

½ cup raw brown rice
1 cup water or weak broth

CARBOHYDRATES GRAMS
¼ cup cooked rice **9.3**

Rinse and drain rice. Bring water or broth to a boil. Add rice, cover, and allow to simmer for 45 minutes or until fluffy. (Pot should have a tight-fitting lid.) If after 45 minutes the rice still seems tough, add additional boiling water, cover, and continue cooking. Do not stir. Yield: 1¼ cups.

Note: Candida patients should limit themselves to ¼ cup per meal of any cooked whole grain.

GREEN RICE

This is an attractive way to serve rice on a hot summer day.

1 cup (packed) parsley or watercress (or ¾ cup parsley and ¼ cup watercress)
¼ cup cilantro or dill weed or fennel
2 tablespoons green onion
1 cup brown rice, cooked and chilled
1 tablespoon olive oil
1 tablespoon lemon juice

CARBOHYDRATES	GRAMS
parsley	**5.1**
herbs	**1.0**
green onion	**1.0**
rice	**37.0**
olive oil	**0**
lemon juice	**1.2**
	45.3
per serving	**11.3**

Run greens through food processor or mince finely with a sharp knife. Mix with rice. Pour olive oil and lemon juice over mixture and stir. Serves four. Limit yourself to one serving.

KASHA (BUCKWHEAT GROATS)

2 tablespoons butter
½ cup buckwheat groats
1 cup water

CARBOHYDRATES	GRAMS
¼ cup serving	**8.0**

Melt butter and stir in buckwheat groats. Bring water to boil and pour over groats. Simmer 15 minutes. Serves five.

Variation: Add ¼ cup onions to melted butter.

LENTIL DELIGHT

¼ cup butter
½ cup diced onions
1 cup lentil sprouts or 1 cup lentils
    measured after soaking overnight
½ cup diced celery
½ cup diced bell pepper

CARBOHYDRATES	GRAMS
butter	.4
onions	7.5
celery	2.5
bell pepper	1.9
lentils	about 40.0
	52.3
per serving	13.1

Melt butter over low heat in a heavy pan. Add onions and stir. Add lentils, celery and peppers and cover with a tight lid. Simmer until lentils are fork-tender. Serves four.

MILLET

2 cups water
⅔ cup millet

CARBOHYDRATES	GRAMS
¼ cup cooked millet	14

Bring water to a boil and stir in millet. Cover pot and simmer 20 to 30 minutes. Millet should be fluffy. Yield: approximately 2 cups.

HOMEMADE POTASSIUM BAKING POWDER

1 cup arrowroot flour
1 cup cream of tartar
½ cup potassium bicarbonate (purchase from pharmacy)

CARBOHYDRATES	GRAMS
1 tablespoon	**7**
1 teaspoon	**approx. 2**

Sift ingredients together and store in a tightly closed jar. Sift again before using and use in the same proportions as commercial baking powder.

MILLET MUFFINS

1 cup freshly ground millet flour*
1 cup carrots, grated fine
1 teaspoon kelp powder
2 tablespoons butter
1 teaspoon potassium baking powder (see above)
¾ cup boiling water
3 eggs, separated
2 tablespoons water
¼ teaspoon maple extract

CARBOHYDRATES	GRAMS
millet	**170.0**
kelp	**1.8**
carrots	**11.0**
butter	**.2**
eggs	**1.5**
	184.5
per muffin	**15.4**

Preheat oven to 375°F. Mix flour, carrots, kelp, butter and baking powder. Pour the boiling water over this mixture and stir. Separate eggs. Add water to the beaten egg yolks and add this to the flour mixture. Fold in the stiffly beaten egg whites and maple extract. Fill well-buttered muffin tins ¾ full. Bake for 25 minutes or until golden brown. Makes one dozen muffins.

*Grind ¼ cup millet at a time either in a blender or in a mini-mill.

OAT BRAN CRACKERS

¼ cup boiling water
2 teaspoons butter
½ cup oat bran
salt to taste

CARBOHYDRATES	GRAMS
butter	.1
oat bran	**24.0**
each cracker	**12.0**

Preheat oven to 350°F. Pour boiling water over butter and oat bran. Add salt and mix well with a fork. Shape dough into two balls, and press each into a round flat cracker with your palms and lay them on greased cookie sheet. Bake 20 to 25 minutes, or until light brown. Serve hot with a pat of butter. Yield: two crackers 3½ inches in diameter.

OAT BRAN-SWEET POTATO MUFFINS

2½ cups grated raw sweet potato
2½ cups oat bran
1 tablespoon baking powder (see page 66)
1 teaspoon cinnamon
¼ teaspoon allspice
1 cup water
3 eggs, separated
2 tablespoons melted butter

CARBOHYDRATES	GRAMS
sweet potato	**70.0**
oat bran	**12.0**
spices	**1.0**
eggs	**1.5**
butter	**.2**
12 muffins	**192.7**
each muffin appr.	**16**

Preheat oven to 400° F. Scrub, peel and grate the sweet potato or put through food processor. Grate enough to fill 2½ cups. Place sweet potato in mixing bowl and add oat bran. Add baking powder, cinnamon and allspice. Mix well. Make a depression in the center of this mixture and add water, egg yolks and melted butter. Beat egg whites and fold into batter. Fill 12 greased muffin cups. Bake for 20 to 25 minutes or until a toothpick inserted into the muffin comes out clean. Freeze the leftover muffins at once. One muffin per meal for Candida patients.

SWEET POTATO-OAT BRAN PANCAKES

1 egg
1 medium size sweet potato, peeled,
    scrubbed and cubed
2 tablespoons oat bran
¼ teaspoon potassium baking powder (see
    page 66)
2 tablespoons butter

CARBOHYDRATES	GRAMS
egg	**.4**
sweet potato	**33.0**
oat bran	**6.0**
baking powder	**1.0**
	40.0
each	**10.0**

Place egg in blender and turn to low speed. Gradually add small amounts of sweet potato. Continue blending, and add the oat bran and baking powder. When mixture is smooth and thick, spoon into melted butter in skillet and sauté until lightly browned on each side. Top with additional butter and serve. Makes four pancakes.

POTATO PANCAKES

1 egg
2 small potatoes, scrubbed and cubed
1 slice onion
2 or more parsley sprigs
2 tablespoons oat bran
⅛ tablespoon potassium baking powder (see page 66)
2 tablespoons butter

CARBOHYDRATES	GRAMS
egg	approx .4
2 potatoes	34.2
onion	.8
parsley	.4
oat bran	6.0
butter	.2
baking powder	—
	42.0
per serving	14 or 21

Blend egg, potatoes, onion, and parsley on low speed until finely chopped. Add oat bran and baking powder. Blend on slow speed until well mixed. Melt butter in skillet until just golden. Do not let it turn brown. Sauté by dropping a serving-spoon-size pancake into the melted butter and cooking until golden brown on each side. Serves two or three.

WAFFLES

3 eggs, separated
⅓ cup water
1½ teaspoons vanilla
1 cup arrowroot flour or oat bran or rice flour or mixture of flour, bran and polishings from rice

CARBOHYDRATES	GRAMS
eggs	1.2
vanilla	0.0
arrowroot (1)	112.0
oat bran (2)	48.0
rice flour (3)	85.0
(1)	113.2
(2)	49.2
(3)	86.2
per waffle	
(1)	28.3
(2)	12.3
(3)	21.5

Separate the eggs. Pour the yolks into the blender. Add water and the vanilla to the yolks. Spoon in flour and blend until smooth. Beat egg whites until stiff. Fold the blended mixture into the egg whites until lightly mixed. Spoon into waffle iron and bake until brown. Serve with butter. Eat only one waffle, and consider it as a bread or toast substitute, minus any sweeteners. Makes four waffles.

MEATS AND POULTRY

In addition to a wide assortment of fresh vegetables, a variety of meats, poultry and seafood is included in your modified diet plan.

Pork is omitted since many nutritionists advise against it, especially for a therapeutic diet.

In addition to starving the Candida in your body, you need to rebuild damaged tissue as rapidly as possible. Overcooking meat damages the protein value of the food, makes it less usable and also renders fat indigestible. For specific and comprehensive cooking instructions on meat preparation, there are several excellent books, including Adelle Davis's *Let's Cook It Right*.[15] This has explicit instructions for a method of "slow cooking" meats and poultry, with charts for cooking times and temperatures for different cuts of meats. Another good book is the *Natural Foods Primer*[16] by Beatrice Trum Hunter, which provides handy tips on proper storing and freezing of meats to ensure retention of valuable nutrients. You may also refer to James Beard's *Theory and Practice of Good Cooking*, [17] Beard's *Fish Cookery*,[18] and Irma S. Rombauer and Marion Rombauer Becker's *Joy of Cooking*[19] for comprehensive food preparation advice.

Dos and Don'ts

Variety meats such as kidney, heart and tongue are recommended on a healing diet because they contain exceptional nutrient qualities. However, they spoil quickly and must be used when fresh. Slow cooking is best.

Try to buy poultry that is raised locally and is free of preservatives. Use only freshly purchased meats. Ground meat is more likely to contain mold contaminants, and even after cooking some harmful microorganisms are not destroyed.

Barbecuing and frying are very popular cooking methods, but should be avoided. When meat is barbecued, the smoke produced from the fats splattering on the meat from the hot coals is carcinogenic. Nor are fried foods advisable for Candida patients.[20] Dried, pickled and smoked foods are also inadvisable, as they are more likely to have molds. Lightly salting meat at the table is acceptable.

Equipment

A nested set of stainless steel measuring cups and spoons is necessary for the Rainbow portions. Try the ⅛ cup scoop for smaller portions. (This is the size used for ground coffee.)

A meat thermometer is essential for cooking meats properly. It should be inserted into the meat, away from the bone, to determine the internal temperature of the meat as it cooks.

A crockpot is useful for long, slow cooking. Soups or stews can cook for hours at low temperatures, making it possible if you are away all day, to have the dish completely cooked when you come home.

Stainless steel cooking utensils and one or more stainless steel steamer baskets are recommended to prepare a variety of vegetables for each meal. The pot with a snug cover or vapor seal lid will conduct heat evenly.

An electric blender helps prepare sauces and dressings.

Several sharp knives are essential to cut vegetables, trim fat and test meat for doneness.

A small toaster/broiler oven is handy to bake chicken, fish, steaks and chops. Some of these ovens cook more rapidly than conventional ones.

In any method used to prepare meat, *don't overcook!* If you cook frozen meat, plan to thaw the day of cooking by setting it out in the refrigerator overnight for the next day.

When broiling steaks, place a 1-inch steak approximately 2 inches from the heat source for 3 to 4 minutes per side for medium rare. If using thicker cuts, cook to an internal temperature of 130°F. to 135°F.

Broil a 1-inch lamb chop 2 inches from the heat source for 3 to 4 minutes per side for medium rare. The juices should run pink, as *all* meats continue to cook for several minutes after broiling or roasting.

Broil chicken bone side up first, 4 inches from the heat source for approximately 14 minutes per side. When the juices run clear the chicken should be ready to eat. Of course, the thickness and boniness of a chicken may alter the cooking time slightly.

An old French proverb states, "Cooks are made, roasters

are born." Roast your meat at a low temperature (300°F. to 325°F.) throughout the cooking process. Check its internal temperature with a meat thermometer to determine doneness. The temperatures below are for rare meat. Remember, meats continue to cook for 10 to 15 minutes after they are removed from the oven.

Beef	125°F. to 130°F.	Place thermometer in center cut of chop or steak.
Lamb	130°F. to 135° F.	
Chicken	160°F. to 165°F.	
Turkey	170°F. to 175°F.	Place thermometer in thickest part of thigh for poultry, but not next to the bone.
(unstuffed)		

BROILED CHICKEN

1 chicken, quartered
¼ cup lemon juice
¼ cup olive oil
1 clove garlic crushed
1 inch piece of fresh ginger, grated

CARBOHYDRATES GRAMS
negligible

Rinse chicken and pat dry with paper towels. Marinate in lemon juice, oil, garlic and ginger for one to three hours. Turn oven to broil. Brush chicken with marinade. Place on baking sheet, cut side up. Broil quickly, about 10 minutes. Turn with tongs and place skin side up. Baste again and *bake* about 20 minutes at 450°F.

ROAST TURKEY

12 to 14 pound turkey (free of additives)
juice of 1 or 2 lemons
celery stalks, onion slices
¼ pound or more butter, melted
salt

CARBOHYDRATES GRAMS
negligible

Preheat oven to 325°F. Rinse turkey gently and pat dry with paper towels. Remove liver, heart and gizzard from cavity and steam with the neck, a stalk of celery and slice of onion. (Broth may be added to gravy or frozen for soup.) Remove all fat from cavity and render over low heat while preparing the bird as follows.

Rub the interior cavity with lemon juice. Place a stalk of celery and slice of onion in the cavity. Truss the turkey with twine to close the cavity securely. In a 2-cup measuring cup, pour rendered fat and enough melted butter to make one cup. To this mixture add 4 teaspoons of broth from the organ meat and salt to taste. Coat one side of the bird with ½ of the butter mixture and place it, buttered side up, on a rack in a shallow roasting pan. Roast 1 hour. With hands protected by mitts, turn the turkey to the other side and coat with remaining butter mixture. Roast for 1 hour more. Turn breast side up and baste with juice. Roast for another 25 minutes. Test for doneness by placing thermometer in the thickest part of the thigh (it should register 170–175°F.) or by testing the legs to see if they move easily.

If you have used a fresh turkey and have a generous amount left over, you may choose to strip it from the bones and make broth from the carcass. Then freeze the leftover turkey in broth in individual serving-size packages which can be reheated quickly. Later you can use the defrosted turkey and broth in "Leftover Turkey Curry" or stir-fry recipes.

TURKEY GRAVY

Dissolve 1 tablespoon arrowroot in ¼ cup cooked broth. Add 2 cups of turkey juices. Heat until arrowroot thickens and clears. Add seasonings and a bit of chopped onion for flavor. Makes 2 cups.

CARBOHYDRATES	GRAMS
per 2 cups	**8.0**
per ¼ cup	**1.0**

STOVETOP HOLIDAY DRESSING

2 tablespoons turkey fat or butter
1 cup onions, chopped
2 cups celery, chopped (include leaves)
1 cup carrots, chopped
2 cups zucchini, chopped
1 cup rice, cooked (in broth, if possible)
giblets, cooked and chopped
½ teaspoon dried or 1 tablespoon fresh sage
½ teaspoon dried or 1 tablespoon fresh thyme
salt and/or kelp to taste

CARBOHYDRATES	GRAMS
butter	.2
onion	15.0
celery	10.0
brown rice	37.0
giblets	3.0
herbs	.6
carrots	11.0
zucchini	12.4
Total	89.2
per serving	22.3

Soften onions in fat over low heat. Add celery, carrots and zucchini and simmer until softened. Add rice, giblets and seasonings. Allow to warm. Serves four.

TO BALANCE MEAL: Serve with turkey and lots of other vegetables. It is recommended that you not stuff turkey with dressing.

Note: Candida patients must limit themselves to one serving of dressing and are advised to skip potatoes at this meal—even at Thanksgiving dinner!

TURKEY HASH

1 tablespoon butter
½ cup onions, chopped
½ cup potato, chopped
¾ cup celery, sliced
½ cup bell pepper, chopped
¼ cup carrots, sliced
¾ cup cooked turkey, cubed
broth if desired
½ cup parsley, finely chopped
salt and/or kelp to taste
cayenne pepper or paprika, optional

CARBOHYDRATES	GRAMS
butter	.2
onions	7.5
potato	12.8
celery	5.0
bell pepper	1.9
carrots	3.0
turkey	0.0
parsley	2.5
	33.0
per serving	16.5

Melt butter over low heat. Sauté onions and potatoes. When soft, stir in the remaining vegetables (except parsley), turkey, and broth if desired, and cook gently until just slightly crisp. Add parsley and seasoning. Serves two.

Variations: This recipe calls for leftover frozen turkey, but you can also use other leftover meat, chicken, fish or fresh meats. However, fresh meats should be added before potato is finished cooking.

Note: Candida patients should omit beans and grains when eating potatoes.

LEFTOVER TURKEY CURRY

(Mock Stir-Fry)
This is a good way to use leftover turkey that you have frozen in small packages.

2 tablespoons butter
¾ cup onions, cut in slivers
2 slices ginger root
1 clove garlic, cut in half
1 teaspoon curry powder
6 tablespoons turkey broth
¾ cup bell pepper, cut in slivers
½ cup cooked rice (optional)
¾ cup leftover turkey, torn into bite-size pieces
1 cup bok choy leaves, cut into strips
¾ cup snow peas
¾ cup jicama or water chestnuts, cut into strips

CARBOHYDRATES	GRAMS
butter	.2
onions	10.0
ginger	0.8
garlic	.4
curry	1.0
broth	0.0
pepper	2.5
rice	18.5
turkey	0.0
bok choy	7.0
peas	8.0
jicama	19.2
with rice	67.2
without rice	49.1
per serving with rice	33.8
per serving without rice	24.5

Melt butter in large skillet over low heat. Cut onion in quarters the long way, and cut slivers from the quarters. Sauté onion, ginger root and garlic. Remove garlic and ginger. Add curry powder, broth, and bell pepper strips. When broth has warmed, add rice, turkey pieces and bok choy and cover pan. When bok choy has wilted, add snow peas and jicama and warm for a minute or so. Serves two generously.

Note: This method is preferable to stir-frying. Except for the onion, these vegetables are being warmed rather than cooked to retain their nutrients.

BROILED BUTTERFLIED LAMB LEG

one leg of lamb*
several cloves of garlic
rosemary and marjoram
2 tablespoons butter

CARBOHYDRATES GRAMS
negligible

Cream seasoning in butter and spread on non-fat side of meat. Broil about 5 inches from heat for 15 minutes per side. The lamb should be pink inside, not brown or gray, when done. Slice and serve as you would a steak.

*Ask the butcher to butterfly the lamb to lie flat like steak.

IRISH STEW

½ cup water
¾ cup lamb, cut in 2-inch cubes
½ cup potato, sliced
½ cup carrots, sliced
¾ cup onions, sliced
½ cup green beans, chopped
1 clove garlic, minced
1 bay leaf (small)
¾ cup celery, sliced
¼ teaspoon dried rosemary
½ teaspoon dried mint
¼ teaspoon dried marjoram
2 tablespoons arrowroot
½ cup water

CARBOHYDRATES	GRAMS
lamb	0.0
potato	12.8
carrots	7.0
onions	10.0
green beans	4.0
garlic	.9
celery	4.0
arrowroot	14.0
	52.7
per serving	26.3

Bring water to a boil over medium heat. Add lamb, vegetables and herbs, lower heat and cook until meat is tender. Mix arrowroot with water and turn heat back up to medium. Move vegetables to sides of pan and stir arrowroot into broth. Continue to stir until sauce is thickened. Turn off heat and stir vegetables gently into sauce. Remove bay leaf. Serves two.

LAMB KABOBS

Marinade:

1 tablespoon lemon juice
2 tablespoons olive oil
1 teaspoon dried or 1 tablespoon fresh rosemary or mint, crushed
1 clove garlic, crushed

Kabobs:

¾ cup onions, cut in quarters
¾ cup lamb, cut into 1-inch squares
½ cup green pepper, cut in 1-inch squares
¾ cup cherry tomatoes
½ cup zucchini, cut in 1-inch pieces
½ cup rice, cooked
¼ cup parsley, scissor-snipped

CARBOHYDRATES	GRAMS
lemon juice	1.2
olive oil	0.0
herbs	.8
garlic	.9
lamb	0.0
onions	12.0
green pepper	1.9
tomato	7.5
zucchini	2.8
rice	19.1
parsley	1.4
	47.6
per serving	23.8

Marinate lamb squares for at least 3 hours in a glass or stainless steel dish in refrigerator, turning several times. Pour ¼ cup boiling water over onions to soften, if desired. Cut onion quarters in half again. Thread meat alternately with vegetables onto skewers. Baste meat and vegetables with marinade. Broil for a short time so that meat remains rare and vegetables crunchy. In small saucepan, warm remainder of marinade. (It contains nutritious juices from lamb.) Spoon rice onto two plates and pour marinade over rice, topping with sprinkling of parsley. Place kabobs on bed of rice. Serves two.

Note: Cubes of fish, beef or chicken liver may also be used. If chicken is used, be sure to cut it into thin strips and to cook it until done.

LAMB SAUSAGE

1 pound ground lamb or beef
¼ teaspoon oregano or other herbs to taste
¼ teaspoon sage
¼ teaspoon thyme
1 clove garlic, pressed

CARBOHYDRATES	GRAMS
	negligible

Mix the spices into 2 tablespoons water. Knead this mixture into the ground meat and shape into patties. Broil or pan fry patties to taste. Freeze any not used at once.

BEEF-RUTABAGA STEW

¾ cup beef, cubed
½ cup water or broth
½ cup rutabaga, cut in half and sliced thin
½ cup green beans or celery, sliced
½ cup onions, chopped
1½ cups cabbage, shredded
3 tablespoons parsley, snipped (optional)
½ teaspoon dried or 1 tablespoon fresh basil leaves
½ cup cooked rice (optional)
salt or kelp as desired

CARBOHYDRATES	GRAMS
beef	0.0
rutabaga	7.7
green beans	4.0
onions	7.0
cabbage	9.0
parsley	1.0
herbs	.5
rice	19.1
	48.3
per serving	24.1

Put beef, water or broth, rutabaga, green beans, onions and cabbage in pot. Cover with lid and bring just barely to a boil over medium heat. Reduce heat and simmer for 12 to 15 minutes, or until tender and crunchy. Turn off heat and stir in rice, herbs and seasoning. Cover pot and allow stew to sit a few minutes. Serves two.

Variation: Substitute any beans or other grain for rice, and experiment with all kinds of vegetables.

CHILI CON CARNE

1 or 2 cloves garlic, minced
¾ cup onions, chopped
¼ cup broth from beans or leftovers
1 cup beef, cut into cubes
1 cup cooked kidney beans
1 cup bell pepper, chopped
1 cup chopped celery, including tops and
    outer stalks
2 tablespoons tomato paste, optional
2 to 4 teaspoons chili powder
2 teaspoons cumin, optional
1 teaspoon dried oregano, optional
1½ cups tomatoes, chopped
2 tablespoons olive oil

CARBOHYDRATES	GRAMS
garlic	1.8
onions	12.0
beef	0.0
beans	42.0
bell pepper	3.8
celery	5.0
tomato paste	6.0
herbs	4.5
tomatoes	15.0
olive oil	0.0
four servings	90.1
per serving	22.5

Cook garlic and onions in broth over low heat until onions begin to soften. Add beef cubes and cook briefly. Add kidney beans, bell peppers, celery and more liquid if desired. Cook until beef is tender. Stir in tomato paste, spices and tomatoes and let warm. Stir in olive oil and let sit a few moments to blend flavors. Serves three or four.

Variation: Sauté onions and garlic in 2 tablespoons butter and omit olive oil.

For a balanced meal: Serve with romaine lettuce salad and French dressing. Freeze any leftover chili for another time.

TOSTADAS

2 corn tortillas
1 cup lettuce, shredded, or alfalfa sprouts
¾ cup beef, cut in ½- or ¾-inch cubes and
    sautéed lightly
¾ cup tomato, chopped
¼ cup green onion, chopped
¼ cup cilantro leaves (optional)
½ cup cucumber, peeled and sliced
½ cup carrots, cut in strips

CARBOHYDRATES	GRAMS
tortillas	27.0
beef	0.0
lettuce	1.4
tomato	7.5
green onion	2.0
cilantro	.5
carrots	5.5
cucumbers	1.0
	45.7
per serving	22.8

Moisten tortillas in a little water and warm in toaster oven. (Or you can warm tortillas in a little butter over low heat.) Lay 1 tortilla on each plate. Spread lettuce over tortillas. Spoon beef, tomatoes, green onions and cilantro over lettuce. Serve with cucumber slices and carrot strips. Serves two.

Variation: You may add avocado slices or hot chili peppers to the tostada.

Note: Candida patients should limit themselves to 1 tortilla at a meal.

KIDNEY STEW

2 tablespoons butter
¼ teaspoon rosemary
¼ teaspoon marjoram
4 to 5 lambs' kidneys, sliced thin
½ green pepper, sliced
½ onion, sliced
2 stalks celery, sliced
extra broth, if necessary
1 tablespoon arrowroot to each 1½ cups
  juice

CARBOHYDRATES	GRAMS
butter	.2
green pepper	2.0
onion	3.0
celery	4.0
herbs +	
kidneys	negligible
arrowroot	7.0
	16.2
per serving	8.1

Melt butter and add rosemary and marjoram. Add kidneys, green pepper, onion and celery. Stir-fry until warmed through (3 to 4 minutes). Add extra broth, if necessary. Mix arrowroot with a little water and add to broth. Continue stirring until clear. Season with herbed salt and serve. Serves two.

COOKED TONGUE

1 large calf or beef tongue or
1 to 2 small lamb tongues per person
water to cover
8 peppercorns
2 medium onions, halved
4 carrots
several celery tops
4 new potatoes or Jerusalem artichokes

CARBOHYDRATES	GRAMS
tongue	0.0
onions	12.0
carrots	30.0
celery	2.0
potatoes	45.0
	89.0
per serving	22.2

Place tongue in a Dutch oven. Add water and peppercorns to pot and bring to simmer (when the lid dances). Turn heat as low as possible. Cook at low heat approximately two hours for beef tongue, under two hours for lamb. Add all vegetables for the last half hour of cooking, taking care not to overcook. Save the broth, which is rich in minerals. Serves four or more, depending on the size of the tongue.

SEAFOOD

The classical Chinese philosopher Lao-tzu said, "Ruling a large kingdom is like cooking a small fish." Both should be gently handled and their treatment never overdone!

Seafood is high in trace minerals and is an excellent source of protein. Fish from deep ocean waters are most desirable, as they are freer from pollutants than fresh-water fish or scavengers. When shopping for fish, seek a local fish market. Fresh fish should have little or no odor and a bright sheen. The flesh should be firm, the eyes bulging. Fish on the bone retains more of its natural juices than when filleted. Culinary artist James Beard recommends cooking fish with its head and tail intact and claims it is more flavorful this way.[21]

Fresh fish is highly perishable. It must be used at once or frozen promptly. In freezing, place fish in a plastic bag and squeeze out as much air as possible to prevent dryness. Fish can be stored in the freezer of a refrigerator for only a week or two because such freezers are not sufficiently cold to prevent enzymatic changes that make nutritional value and flavor decline. If you have a deep freezer, remember that oily fish (such as salmon) do not store as long as other fish.

When thawing fish, allow about eight hours per pound in the lower compartment of your refrigerator. A slow-thawing process will retain more of the natural juices. Pieces of frozen fish, which cook quickly, can be added to soups and stews.

Fish requires briefer cooking time than meats. The connective tissues of fish are delicate and break down quickly when heated. Because there is very little fat, heat penetrates more rapidly. Seasonings other than salt should be added at the beginning of the cooking process. A court bouillon (fish broth) can be prepared by lightly poaching a portion of fish seasoned with salt and other seasonings and then freezing the broth for later use.

Broiling is most appropriate for fish steaks or fillets (1 inch or more), approximately 5 minutes per side. Thinner pieces or fillets can be braised or poached in water or court bouillon. Poaching is most successful if the fish is placed over water on a flat steamer rack or wrapped in cheesecloth. This prevents the fish from flaking when removed from the broth.

To check for doneness, cut into the fish. No translucent flesh should be seen. Check about a minute before you think the fish will be done. If you wait until the fish falls apart at the touch of a fork, it will be overdone. If you are using a meat thermometer, the internal temperature should be 140° F to 145° F.

Fish is often served with a sauce containing olive oil or avocado. Make your own tartar sauce or mayonnaise, or prepare a cooked sauce with sautéed herbed onions and garlic in butter.

Make a colorful fish entree by shredding vegetables (carrots, onions, celery and zucchini) into a Pyrex baking dish that has been lightly coated with olive oil. Place fish portions on top of this bed of vegetables, lightly brush the fish with herbed butter and bake it at 325° F. until done.

BASIC POACHED FISH

This method of cooking fish is suggested for Candida patients. The fish is cooked at a low temperature, which yields a small quantity of delicious concentrated broth. If you do not use a vapor seal lid, increase the water in the recipe.

1 or 2 red snappers, whitefish or bass fillets
pinch thyme
2 tablespoons water or court bouillon
lemon wedges

CARBOHYDRATES   GRAMS
negligible

Rinse fillets, pat dry and season with thyme. Heat water over medium heat until water begins to bubble. Reduce heat and place fish in pot with water or court bouillon. Cover and simmer for 4 minutes, then turn fish and simmer 3 to 4 minutes on other side or until almost done. (Fish will continue to cook after being removed from the heat.) Serve with lemon wedges. Serves two.

Variations: Complete fish with one of the following sauces (see pages 116–121)
Curry Sauce
Tartar Sauce
Salsa de la Cocina
Quick Onion Sauce

EASY HERBED FISH

This is a good way to prepare fish when you don't make a sauce.

1 tablespoon butter
½ teaspoon dried marjoram
½ pound fish (sole, cod, etc.)

CARBOHYDRATES	GRAMS
butter	**.1**
herb	**.5**
fish	**0.0**
per serving	**.6**

Melt butter over low heat. Stir in marjoram. Rinse fish and pat dry with paper towel. Coat both sides of fish with herbed butter and lay in pan. Simmer, covered, about 4 minutes for ⅜-inch-thick fish. Turn and simmer about 3 minutes. Check for doneness. Serves one.

FISH IN BUTTER-GINGER SAUCE

⅔ cup Butter-Ginger Sauce (see page 116)
⅔ pound fish (sole, cod, etc.)

CARBOHYDRATES	GRAMS
sauce per serving	**8.6**
fish	**negligible**

Prepare Butter-Ginger Sauce in saucepan over low heat so as to prevent butter from browning. Rinse fish and drain on paper towel. Lay fish over sauce. Cover pot and simmer a few minutes. Turn fish and cover with sauce. Simmer until almost done. (See instructions on checking for doneness, pages 85–86.) Serves two.

FISH CACCIATORE

¾ cup Cacciatore Sauce (see page 116)
⅔ pound fish (sole, cod, etc.)

CARBOHYDRATES	GRAMS
sauce per serving	**15.6**
fish	**negligible**

Prepare sauce in saucepan. Rinse fish and pat dry with paper towel. Lay fish over sauce and cover pot. Simmer 3 to 4 minutes. Turn fish, cover with sauce and simmer until just done. Serves two.

FISH CHOWDER

3 to 4 tablespoons butter
½ cup leek or onion, minced
1 clove garlic, minced
½ cup thinly sliced carrots
½ cup thinly sliced celery
½ cup thinly sliced red potato
2 cups broth (any kind you have on hand)
¼ cup parsley, chopped
½ bay leaf
1 whole clove
a few celery tops, chopped
¾ cups white fish (sole, bass, etc.) cut into cubes
⅛ teaspoon kelp
⅛ teaspoon sea salt, if desired
2 tablespoons parsley or chives, minced

CARBOHYDRATES	GRAMS
butter	**.4**
onion	**7.0**
garlic	**.5**
carrots	**5.5**
celery	**2.3**
potato	**12.5**
parsley, fish	**1.2**
	27.4
per serving	**13.7**

Melt butter over low heat and add minced leek or onion, garlic, carrots, celery, potato and broth. Cover and simmer until vegetables are partially tenderized, about 5 minutes. Add parsley, bay leaf, clove, celery tops and fish. Simmer 3 minutes more. Add kelp and salt. Remove bay leaf. Serve with snipped parsley or chives. Serves two.

ITALIAN FISH STEW (FOR TWO)

Choose fish with a firm texture. Frozen fish with less attractive appearance than fresh fish may be used. Or you may use scraps, such as the meat from the jaws of the fish.

2 tablespoons butter
1 clove garlic, minced
½ cup onion chopped
½ green pepper, chopped
1 cup celery, chopped
½ cup water or broth
¾ cup raw fish, cut in chunks
¾ cup very ripe tomato
½ cup parsley, coarsely chopped
¼ cup celery leaves, chopped
¼ teaspoon dried oregano
¼ teaspoon dried basil
¼ teaspoon dried thyme
juice of lemon or lime, if desired

CARBOHYDRATES	GRAMS
butter	.2
garlic	.9
onion	7.5
green pepper	1.9
celery	6.3
fish	0.0
tomato	7.5
parsley	2.6
herbs	1.0
lemon juice	3.6
	31.5
per serving	15.8

Melt butter over low heat. Add garlic and onions and continue to cook over low heat, stirring occasionally, until softened. Stir in green pepper, celery, and broth. Continue to cook for 2 minutes. Add fish chunks and cook another few minutes, until fish is almost done. Add tomato, greens and herbs and cook another two minutes. Fish should be cooked through but the vegetables should be still crisp and colorful. Remove from heat, cover, and let sit 3 to 5 minutes. Add lemon or lime juice and serve with yeast-free rye crackers. Serves two generously.

Variations: Stir in precooked beans or rice.
Add ½ cup diced potatoes with onion and cook until soft. If potatoes are added, omit beans and rice.

MOCK TUNA-STUFFED TOMATO

This makes an attractive platter for a warm summer day luncheon.

¾ cup fish, steamed and cooled
¾ cup celery, chopped fine
¾ cup parsley, minced
6 tablespoons green onion, minced
3 or 4 tablespoons Homemade Mayonnaise
(see page 114)
½ teaspoon dried or 1 tablespoon fresh tarragon, snipped
2 tomatoes, cut in wedges
½ teaspoon dried or 1 tablespoon fresh dill weed, snipped

CARBOHYDRATES	GRAMS
fish	0.0
celery	5.7
parsley	3.7
onion	3.0
mayonnaise	0.5
tomatoes	14.0
	26.9
per serving	13.4

Flake fish and mix with chopped vegetables, mayonnaise and tarragon. Arrange tomato wedges in a wheel on two plates. Spoon fish mixture over tomatoes. Garnish with fresh dill weed or lettuce. Serves two.

Variations: Add carrot strips.
Stir cold cooked rice into the fish mixture or serve the salad with yeast-free rye crackers.

VEGETABLES

When purchasing vegetables, seek out the freshest possible, locally organically grown on good soil. Learn when produce is delivered to your market and plan your shopping accordingly.

Give carrots, beets and squash the "pinch test," and reject any with soggy areas. Bypass cauliflower or broccoli that has any discolored or moldy areas. Avoid any potatoes that are green or sprouting due to overexposure to heat or light.

Seasonal produce will have the best flavor and be less expensive. Some additive-free frozen vegetables can be stocked for "emergencies," but plan to shop frequently for the fresh varieties in order to obtain optimal levels of needed vitamins and minerals.

Mold accumulates rapidly on surfaces whether food is refrigerated or not refrigerated. Wash vegetables before you use them rather than before storing them. Then scrub them with a stiff brush.

In storing greens, retain as much moisture in them as possible by dampening and then storing them leafy side down in plastic bags tied with a twister. Allow some air to remain inside of the bag before closing it to prevent the greens from becoming soggy.

Cut the leaves and stems from carrots and beets. This will prevent moisture and nutrients from being drawn out. Store the greens in separate bags. Store celery with a plastic bag protecting its green leaves. Zucchini and eggplant store best when left unwrapped in the refrigerator crisper drawer. Cauliflower stores best in the perforated wrapper that is kept slightly loose. Store onions, potatoes, yams and winter squash in a cool cupboard with plenty of air circulation.

Scrub vegetables with a stiff brush before preparing. Avoid soaking, which results in the loss of nutrients in the water which is discarded. Do not peel vegetables if the peel is edible. It contains nutrients and dietary fibers. Nearly all vegetables except leafy greens can be saved for another recipe merely by cutting off the exposed ends before using them on another occasion.

Grate, mash or puree at the very last minute in order to prevent nutrient losses. As you become more experienced with minimal cooking times and use of very little liquid for cooking, you will better appreciate the brilliant colors and savory flavors in vegetable dishes.

Do not precook vegetables for future use; instead, cut the dense varieties into small pieces to cook in the same amount of time as other ingredients. Save the cooking liquids and add them to recipes requiring liquids, preserving the water-soluble nutrients.

GLOBE ARTICHOKES

If you've never eaten an artichoke before, try it—it's fun! Just pull an outside artichoke leaf, dip in the butter and pull the "meat" off the leaf with your teeth. When you reach the center, carefully remove and discard the thistles with a spoon and eat the heart.

globe artichokes
softened or melted butter or Homemade
  Mayonnaise (see page 114)

CARBOHYDRATES	GRAMS
1 artichoke	**9.9**
mayonnaise	**1.2**
	11.1

Select artichokes with tightly closed leaves. Cut off stem, rinse well. Cover and cook in a little water over low heat 30 to 40 minutes, depending on size. Stand the artichoke upright on plate and serve with a small cup of softened or melted butter, or homemade mayonnaise.

Note: In cooking for one, you may prefer to cook half an artichoke at a time. Simply cut it downward in half with a sharp knife and cook as above. In preparing a Super Seven Meal, tear off a handful of leaves at a time and cook them with the other vegetables. When you have used up all the outer leaves, cook the heart, remove and discard the delicate inner leaves and thistles and then either eat the heart as is or put it in a salad.

Variation: add lemon juice to melted butter.

CAULIFLOWER-EGGPLANT CURRY

1 tablespoon butter
½ teaspoon curry powder
1½ cups small cauliflower florets
1 cup eggplant, chopped
½ cup fresh peas
½ cup tomato, chopped
2 teaspoons lemon juice
2 tablespoons water (or more if not using vapor seal lid)

CARBOHYDRATES	GRAMS
butter	.1
curry	.5
cauliflower	9.0
eggplant	8.0
peas	9.5
tomato	7.0
lemon	.4
	34.5
per serving	17.2
Variation:	
rice, ½ cup	18.0
per serving	9.0

Melt butter over low heat and stir in curry powder. Add cauliflower and stir to coat. Add eggplant and peas. Add water and cover pot. Cook over medium heat just long enough to bring to a boil. Reduce heat and simmer until tender, about 8 minutes. Remove from heat and stir in tomatoes and lemon juice. Serves two.

Variation: Substitute zucchini for eggplant; substitute green beans, cut in ½-inch pieces, for peas. Before adding tomato, stir in ½ cup cooked brown rice.

CROWNED EGGPLANT

1 eggplant
2 large tomatoes, sliced
1 large onion, sliced thin
1 cup parsley, minced fine
2 to 3 tablespoons fresh basil, minced (optional)
2 tablespoons butter

CARBOHYDRATES	GRAMS
eggplant	**16.0**
tomatoes	**18.0**
onion	**10.9**
butter	**.2**
parsley, basil	**5.1**
	50.2
per serving	**8.4**

Butter a cookie sheet and arrange eggplant slices on it. Place an onion slice and a tomato slice on each piece of eggplant. Add ½ teaspoon butter or less to each stack of vegetables. Bake at 350° for 15 minutes or until fork-tender and soft. Garnish with herbs. A medium eggplant usually gives 12 slices or 6 servings. Prepare only the number of stacks of vegetables needed for one meal.

BAKED "FRENCH FRIES"

A delicious substitute for french fried potatoes.
1 medium potato
½ tablespoon butter or oil

CARBOHYDRATES	GRAMS
potato	**21.0**
per serving	**10.5**

Preheat oven to 450° F. Scrub potato, cut into slices, and then into ½ inch sticks, with skins retained. Arrange in one layer in baking pan. Brush with melted butter or oil. Bake for 15 minutes or until potato sticks are puffed and golden brown. Serves two.

RATATOUILLE

2 cloves garlic, minced
1 cup onions, chopped
2 tablespoons water (or more if needed)
2 cups eggplant, peeled and chopped
2 cups zucchini, chopped
1 cup bell pepper, chopped
¼ cup green onions, chopped
2 cups tomatoes, chopped
1 cup parsley, chopped
1 cup celery leaves, chopped
2 tablespoons tomato paste (optional)
½ teaspoon dried or 1 tablespoon fresh basil
½ teaspoon dried or 1 tablespoon fresh oregano
½ teaspoon dried or 1 tablespoon fresh thyme
2 tablespoons olive oil
salt and/or kelp, if desired

CARBOHYDRATES	GRAMS
garlic	1.8
eggplant	14.8
onions	15.0
zucchini	11.0
bell pepper	3.8
green onions	2.0
tomato	20.0
parsley	5.1
celery	5.0
herbs	1.5
olive oil	0.0
tomato paste	12.2
	92.2
per serving	15.7

Soften garlic and onions in water over low heat. (Increase water if not using waterless cookware.) Add eggplant and cook until it begins to soften. Add zucchini and cook until soft. Add bell pepper, green onions, tomatoes, parsley, celery leaves, tomato paste and herbs and allow to warm. Add olive oil and let sit a few minutes. (If you like it soupier, add a little water or broth.) Serves six.

MOCK SPAGHETTI

1⅓ cups Cacciatore Sauce (see page 116,
    double quantity)
1 small spaghetti squash

CARBOHYDRATES   GRAMS
cacciatore sauce
w/o tomato paste **27.2**
cacciatore sauce
w/tomato paste **33.30**
spaghetti squash **not
available**

Fill pan with 1½ inches water and bring to a boil over medium
heat. Meanwhile, cut squash lengthwise, and scoop out seeds.
Place squash in pan, cut side down. Cover pot and simmer for
20 to 30 minutes, or until you can puncture squash with a fork.
Remove from heat and pull pulp away from shell. It will look
like spaghetti strings. Spoon Cacciatore Sauce over squash.
Serves two generously.

SALADS

BRUSSELS SPROUTS SALAD

This is a good balance of tender cooked and crunchy raw vegetables.

¾ cup brussels sprouts, quartered
¾ cup green beans, cut in ½-inch pieces
1 cup celery, chopped
½ cup bell pepper, chopped
2 tablespoons green onions, chopped
5 tablespoons olive oil
3 tablespoons lemon juice
2 tablespoons fresh or 1½ teaspoons dried
   basil
¾ cup parsley, chopped

CARBOHYDRATES	GRAMS
brussels sprouts	**7.5**
beans	**6.0**
celery	**6.0**
pepper	**1.9**
onions	**.8**
parsley	**4.0**
lemon	**3.6**
	29.8
per serving	**14.9**
½ cup chickpeas add	**30**
½ cup cooked rice add	**10**

Cook brussels sprouts and green beans until tender but crunchy. Drain and chill one hour. Chop remaining vegetables and combine them with the cooked vegetables. Mix together olive oil, lemon juice and herbs. Shake well and pour over salad. Toss to coat vegetables and chill one to two hours. Serves two generously.

Variation: Add either ½ cup cooked chickpeas or ½ cup cooked rice.

CAESAR SALAD

1 clove garlic, bruised
3 cups romaine lettuce, washed, dried and
   torn
salt to taste
¼ teaspoon dry mustard or to taste
4 anchovy fillets, minced (optional)
juice of 2 lemons
¼ cup olive oil
1 egg

CARBOHYDRATES	GRAMS
garlic	.9
lettuce	6.0
lemon	4.8
egg	.5
	12.2
per serving	6.1
Variation:	
½ cup rice add	19.1

Mash garlic with garlic press or with the flat side of a knife to release oils into salad bowl. Fill salad bowl with lettuce. Sprinkle with salt, dry mustard and anchovies. Add lemon juice and olive oil. Break raw egg over salad. Toss gently until well mixed. Serves two.

Note: Candida patients should not add croutons from yeasted bread. Substitute ½ cup cooked rice or millet or crumbs from a yeast-free bread.

CARROT-CABBAGE SALAD

This is a colorful salad that your guests will enjoy.

1½ cups red cabbage, grated
1 cup carrots, grated
½ cup red bell pepper, grated
2 tablespoons green onions, chopped
Ginger Dressing (see page 113).

CARBOHYDRATES	GRAMS
red cabbage	7.2
carrots	11.0
pepper	1.9
onions	1.5
Ginger Dressing	3.8
	25.4
per serving	12.7

Pour Ginger Dressing over vegetables and toss well. Serves two.

Variation: This salad is also good with Green Goddess Dressing. (see page 114).

CAULIFLOWER-EGG SALAD

3 to 4 hard-cooked eggs, chilled (see page 34)

2 tablespoons water

1½ cups cauliflower, cut very small

½ cup celery, chopped

¼ cup bell pepper, chopped fine

2 tablespoons green onions, chopped fine

½ cup parsley, minced

1 tablespoon thick Homemade Mayonnaise (see page 114)

½ teaspoon dried or 1 sprig fresh tarragon leaves

½ teaspoon dried or 1 tablespoon fresh dill weed

1 teaspoon lemon juice

CARBOHYDRATES	GRAMS
eggs	1.5
cauliflower	9.0
celery	2.5
pepper	.9
scallions	1.5
parsley	2.4
herbs	1.0
lemons	.5
mayonnaise	**negligible**
	19.3
per serving	8.4

Bring 2 tablespoons water to a boil over medium heat and add cauliflower. Reduce heat, cover and simmer until tender, 8 to 10 minutes. Drain cauliflower and chill in covered dish. Peel cooked eggs, dice and chill in covered dish for about one hour. Prepare remaining vegetables and combine with chilled ingredients. Add mayonnaise and seasonings and toss. Serves two.

GINGER CHICKEN SALAD

This recipe is unusual because of the contrast of the warm chicken with the cool salad vegetables.

¼ cup Ginger Dressing (see page 113)
2 tablespoons sesame seeds, optional
2 tablespoons butter
1 clove garlic, minced
1-inch cube ginger, grated
3 half chicken breasts, deboned
2 tablespoons water
3 cups lettuce, torn
1 cup Chinese cabbage, slivered
1 cup parsley, chopped
1 cup celery, sliced
¼ cup green onions, sliced
½ cup red cabbage, slivered

CARBOHYDRATES	GRAMS
sesame seeds	3.0
butter	.2
garlic	.9
ginger	1.3
chicken	0.0
lettuce	6.0
cabbage	2.3
parsley	5.1
celery	5.0
green onions	2.0
cabbage	2.5
Ginger Dressing	4.6
	32.9
per serving	8.1

Prepare Ginger Dressing and let sit. Spread sesame seeds out on a pan and toast in a 250° F. oven about 30 minutes. Melt butter over low heat and sauté garlic and ginger. Cut chicken into bite-size pieces and sauté in butter. Add water, cover pot and cook chicken over low heat until done. Chop vegetables into salad bowl. Add hot chicken to salad. Pour Ginger Dressing over salad and toss. Sprinkle hot sesame seeds over salad and serve at once. Serves four.

Variations:
Cooked peas, avocado cubes or 1 cup of cooked rice may be added.
Cooked turkey can be sautéed for a few minutes and substituted for chicken. Try fish for contrast.
Red onion rings can be substituted for red cabbage.

COLESLAW

1½ cups green cabbage, grated or shredded
½ cup green pepper, chopped
½ cup carrots, grated
¼ cup green onions, chopped
3 or 4 tablespoons Homemade Mayonnaise
(see page 114)
dash lemon juice
¼ teaspoon celery seed or caraway seed,
ground

CARBOHYDRATES	GRAMS
cabbage	9.0
pepper	1.9
carrots	5.5
onions	1.6
celery seed	1.5
lemon	.5
mayonnaise	.7
	20.7
per serving	10.3

Combine prepared vegetables. Mix mayonnaise, lemon juice
and seasoning and pour over vegetables. Toss. Serves two.

Variation: Add anise root slivers and omit celery and caraway
seed from dressing.

FISH SALAD

2 cups salad greens (lettuce, watercress,
etc.)
½ cup grated carrots
¼ cup diced bell pepper
½ cup sliced celery
¼ cup chopped radishes
½ cup fish, cooked and chilled
½ cup rice, cooked and chilled
2 to 3 tablespoons Homemade Mayonnaise
(see page 114)
½ lemon

CARBOHYDRATES	GRAMS
lettuce	4.0
carrots	5.5
pepper	.9
celery	2.5
radish	1.5
rice	20.0
mayonnaise	.3
lemon	2.5
	37.2
per serving	18.6

Layer greens and vegetables on two plates. Mix fish with mayonnaise and add rice. Spoon over vegetables and toss lightly. Squeeze lemon juice over each. Serves two.

Variations:
Mix fresh herbs or curry powder into mayonnaise.
Substitute avocado dressing for mayonnaise.
Substitute any raw vegetables on hand for those listed above.
Lightly cooked peas are especially good in salads.
Substitute millet for rice, or omit the grain altogether.

GARDEN LUNCHEON PLATTER

This makes an attractive platter for a hot summer day.

On each plate arrange:

several sprigs watercress
3 or 4 asparagus spears, cooked and cooled
½ tomato, cut in wedges
2 hard-cooked eggs, sliced in half lengthwise
cucumber strips
carrot strips
small celery stalks from celery heart, with leaves
2 tablespoons Homemade Mayonnaise (see page 114)
fresh chives, parsley, dill or other herbs, minced

CARBOHYDRATES	GRAMS
watercress	.1
asparagus	2.0
tomato	3.5
eggs	.8
cucumber	1.0
carrot	4.0
celery	2.0
parsley	.2
mayonnaise	.4
	14.0
Variation:	
fish, add	10.0
substitutes approx. same	

Arrange first four ingredients on one side of plate and drizzle mayonnaise over them. Arrange finger vegetables on other side of plate. Sprinkle snipped herbs over mayonnaise. The above amounts will serve one person.

Variations: Place ¼ cup cooked, cooled rice in center of plate. Or substitute cooked flaked fish mixed with mayonnaise; substitute green onions for hard-cooked eggs. Substitute lightly cooked broccoli, cauliflower or green beans for asparagus; spinach leaves or alfalfa sprouts for watercress, etc.

GREEN SALAD

A reminder of how lovely a simple green salad can be for entertaining on a hot day.

6 medium-sized romaine leaves, torn
½ cup watercress, torn
½ cup cilantro or parsley, torn
¾ cup Chinese cabbage, slivered
½ cup celery, sliced diagonally
2 or 3 red onion rings, sliced very thin
½ avocado, sliced lengthwise (optional)
olive oil
lemon juice

CARBOHYDRATES	GRAMS
lettuce	**1.0**
parsley	**2.4**
watercress	**1.1**
cabbage	**1.5**
celery	**2.3**
onions	**1.5**
avocado	**6.0**
lemon	**2.0**
	17.8
per serving	**8.9**

Prepare greens in a salad bowl. Add celery and toss. Garnish with onion and avocado. Add olive oil and lemon juice or other favorite dressing. Serves two.

JANE'S SALAD

This salad is attractive when placed on a bed of whole lettuce leaves, garnished with 2 or 3 tomato wedges on the side.

¾ cup cooked turkey, shredded or chopped
½ cup fresh peas, lightly cooked
½ cup celery, chopped
½ cup cauliflower, pulled apart or cut into small pieces
1 tablespoon red onion, chopped
¼ cup parsley, chopped
1 cup lettuce, chopped

CARBOHYDRATES	GRAMS
turkey	**0.0**
peas	**10.0**
celery	**2.5**
cauliflower	**3.0**
onion	**1.0**
parsley	**1.2**
lettuce	**2.0**
	19.7
per serving	**9.8**

Toss with Homemade Mayonnaise (see page 114) or other dressing. Serves two.

Variation: If red onion is unavailable, garnish with bits of red pepper or red cabbage.

MEXICAN SALAD

¾ cup beef, broiled and cut in ½-inch
   squares
1½ cups lettuce, torn
¾ cup tomato, chopped
¾ cup celery, chopped
½ cup green onions, chopped
½ cup cucumber, peeled and chopped
¼ cup fresh cilantro
½ cup avocado, chopped
½ cup pinto beans, cooked and cooled
½ teaspoon chili powder, or to taste
1 tablespoon olive oil
juice of ½ lemon or lime

CARBOHYDRATES	GRAMS
beef	0.0
lettuce	3.0
tomatoes	7.5
celery	3.5
onions	3.0
cucumber	2.0
cilantro	1.2
avocado	8.0
beans	30.0
lemon	2.5
	60.7
per serving	30.3

Combine beef and chopped vegetables in an attractive serving
dish. Sprinkle chili powder over salad. Pour oil and juice over
salad. Toss well. Serves two.

Variation: Add chili peppers if desired.

MINT-PEA SALAD

¼ cup green onions, minced
½ cup peas, fresh or frozen
3 cups loosely packed lettuce, finely torn
1 cup celery, sliced
½ cup loosely packed fresh mint leaves,
   scissor-snipped
2 teaspoons olive oil
2 teaspoons lemon juice

CARBOHYDRATES	GRAMS
onions	2.0
peas	10.0
lettuce	6.0
celery	4.0
mint	1.0
lemon	1.0
	24.0
per serving	12.0

Cook onions and fresh peas in a little water over low heat until they are soft. (If you use frozen peas, defrost and use as they are.) Remove onion and peas from cooking water and let cool. Make a bed of torn lettuce on each plate. Add sliced celery, peas, onions and mint leaves. Spoon mixed oil and lemon juice over each plate. Serves two.

ORIENTAL SALAD

¾ cup chicken, cooked, cooled and cut in cubes
½ cup bell pepper, cut in slivers
½ cup snow peas
½ cup celery, slivered
½ cup bean sprouts
1 cup watercress or parsley, chopped
½ cup jicama, cut into strips
Ginger Dressing (see page 113)

CARBOHYDRATES	GRAMS
pepper	1.9
peas	10.0
celery	2.0
sprouts	2.5
watercress	5.0
jicama	12.8
Ginger Dressing	3.8
	38.0
per serving	19.0

Put chicken and vegetables in salad bowl. Pour Ginger Dressing over salad and toss. Serves two.

Variation: Substitute Jerusalem artichokes or canned water chestnuts for jicama. Garnish with sesame seeds.

CURRIED RICE SALAD

½ cup cooked rice
½ cup cooked peas (or defrosted frozen peas)
1 cup celery, sliced
2 tablespoons green onion, chopped
½ cup bell pepper, chopped
½ cup carrots, sliced
¼ cup Homemade Mayonnaise (see page 114)
1 teaspoon curry powder or to taste

CARBOHYDRATES	GRAMS
rice	**18.5**
peas	**10.0**
celery	**6.0**
onion	**1.0**
pepper	**1.9**
carrots	**8.0**
curry powder	**1.0**
mayonnaise	**.6**
	47.0
per serving	**23.5**

Mix all the ingredients well. Let sit a few minutes to blend the flavors. Serves two.

Variation: Rice cooked in broth adds extra flavor to the salad. Use lightly cooked vegetables if desired. Add or substitute other vegetables, such as Jerusalem artichokes, water chestnuts, tomatoes or zucchini.

STEAK SALAD

½ cup broiled beef (rib steak, etc.) cut in cubes

2 cups lettuce (romaine, etc.) torn, or alfalfa sprouts

½ cup or less rice, cooked and cooled (optional)

½ cup raw carrot, grated

½ cup radishes, sliced

½ cup snow peas

½ cup cucumber, peeled and sliced

salt or kelp if desired

CARBOHYDRATES	GRAMS
beef	0.0
lettuce	4.0
rice	19.1
carrot	5.5
radishes	2.0
snow peas	4.0
cucumber	1.8
Basic French Dressing	2.6
	39.0
per serving	19.5

Chill meat 1 hour. Make a bed of torn lettuce on each plate. Sprinkle rice over lettuce, followed by grated carrot. Add radishes, snow peas, cucumber and meat. Serve with Basic French Dressing (see page 111) with ¼ teaspoon of dry mustard added.

Variations: You can substitute any vegetables you like. Tomatoes, bell pepper, celery, onions, peas and artichoke hearts would be excellent choices.

TABOULI

A grain salad from the Middle East.

¼ cup bulgur wheat
½ cup boiling water
½ cup green onions, chopped
1 cup parsley, chopped
½ cup bell pepper, chopped
1½ cups tomato, chopped
1½ cups celery, chopped
¼ cup fresh mint leaves, finely chopped
2 tablespoons olive oil
¼ cup lemon juice or to taste
salt, if needed
kelp, if desired

CARBOHYDRATES	GRAMS
bulgur	21.2
onions	7.5
parsley, mint, oil	5.0
pepper	1.9
tomato	15.2
celery	7.5
lemon	4.8
	63.1
per serving	15.7

Pour water over the bulgur and let stand for 2 hours until light and fluffy. Remove excess water by draining through a strainer or squeezing with your hands. Mix bulgur with chopped vegetables and mint. Add oil, lemon juice, salt and kelp, and chill 1 hour. Serve with meat, fish or eggs for a balanced meal. Serves four.

Note: Bell pepper and celery are not customarily included in tabouli. If omitted, increase the quantity of other vegetables.

DRESSINGS

ANCHOVY DRESSING

1 can of anchovies in olive oil
1 cup olive oil
1 clove garlic, minced
¼ cup lemon juice
¼ cup cooked beets, optional

CARBOHYDRATES	GRAMS
anchovies	**trace**
olive oil	**trace**
garlic	**.9**
lemon juice	**4.8**
beets	**3.1**
per 1½ cups	**8.8**
per ⅛ cup serving	**.7**

Puree ingredients in blender. Makes 1½ cups. Use over salads.

AVOCADO SALAD DRESSING

1 ripe avocado
1 clove garlic, minced
1 tablespoon fresh lemon juice
salt and/or kelp
herbal seasoning

CARBOHYDRATES	GRAMS
avocado	**12.6**
garlic	**.9**
lemon juice	**1.2**
per ½ cup	**14.7**
per ⅛ cup serving	**3.7**

Blend all ingredients on low speed until smooth and serve over salad. Makes about ½ cup.

Variation: Add Homemade Mayonnaise (see page 114) to taste for a creamy consistency and 1 or 2 teaspoons grated onions. Thin this dressing with a tablespoon or two of olive oil, if desired. Add chopped tomato.

110

CREAMY CUCUMBER DRESSING

¼ cup Homemade Mayonnaise (see page 114)
½ cup cucumber, peeled and cut into chunks
½ teaspoon dried or 1 tablespoon fresh tarragon leaves
½ teaspoon dried dill or 1 tablespoon fresh dill leaves
¼ teaspoon dried mustard
1 teaspoon lemon juice

CARBOHYDRATES	GRAMS
mayonnaise	.6
cucumber	1.8
herbs	1.0
lemon juice	.4
	3.8
per serving	1.9

Blend on low speed in blender. Let sit a few minutes. Pour over salad. Serves two.

BASIC FRENCH DRESSING

3 tablespoons olive oil
1 tablespoon lemon juice
1 clove garlic, crushed
1 pinch dried tarragon or at least a teaspoon of fresh tarragon leaves
a pinch dried or a teaspoon of fresh thyme leaves
a pinch of salt
a dash of kelp

CARBOHYDRATES	GRAMS
olive oil	0.0
lemon juice	1.2
garlic	.9
herbs	.5
per ¼ cup	2.6

Mix well and pour over salad. Makes ¼ cup.

Variations: French dressing is traditionally made with 3 parts oil to 1 part vinegar. Candida patients need to substitute lemon juice for vinegar. You can adjust the amount of lemon juice according to your taste.

Substitute any herbs you prefer. Or use an herbed seasoning salt to replace salt and herbs.

If you cannot tolerate citrus fruit such as lemon juice, substitute a little powdered vitamin C dissolved in water.

EASIEST-EVER FRENCH DRESSING

If you've been pouring commercially prepared dressing over your salad, you may believe that making homemade French dressing is bothersome. If so, the following method will change your belief. After you've made it once or twice and learned to judge quantities, you'll discover that it's really easy, and there's no jar to wash.

Per person

1 tablespoon olive oil
1 teaspoon lemon juice
a pinch each of dried tarragon or other herbs, dried thyme, salt and kelp

CARBOHYDRATES	GRAMS
olive oil	**0.0**
lemon juice	.4
herbs	.5
	.9

Measure oil and lemon juice and pour into bottom of salad bowl. Toss in herbs and seasonings. Blend with a fork. Add torn lettuce and other salad vegetables. When ready to serve, toss well.

Note: You can also pour the ingredients over the salad and toss. However, the above method allows the herbs to release their flavor into the dressing.

GARBANZO DRESSING

Create a tasty dressing from beans, and use it in place of your bean or grain portion. Bean dressings are high in carbohydrates. Limit portions.

¼ cup cooked garbanzo beans (chickpeas)
¾ cup parsley, chopped
1 tablespoon green onion, chopped
2 tablespoons cooking water from garbanzo beans
2 tablespoons olive oil
1 teaspoon lemon juice
¼ teaspoon dried or 1 tablespoon fresh basil leaves

CARBOHYDRATES	GRAMS
garbanzos	15.0
parsley	4.0
green onion	.5
olive oil	0.0
lemon juice	1.2
herbs	.3
	21.0
per serving	10.5

Puree at low speed in blender. Pour over salad. Serves two.

GINGER DRESSING

3 tablespoons olive oil
1 to 2 tablespoons lemon juice
1 teaspoon freshly grated ginger
1 clove garlic

CARBOHYDRATES	GRAMS
olive oil	0.0
lemon juice	2.4
ginger	.5
garlic	.9
	3.8

Mix and let sit a few minutes. Pour over salad or cooked vegetables. Makes ¼ cup.

GREEN GODDESS DRESSING

¼ cup Homemade Mayonnaise (see below)
1 tablespoon each scissor-snipped parsley,
   chives or green onion, fresh dill leaves or
   ½ teaspoon dried dill weed
1 to 2 teaspoons lemon juice
1 to 2 teaspoons olive oil

CARBOHYDRATES	GRAMS
mayonnaise	.6
parsley	.6
chives	.6
lemon juice	.8
olive oil	0.0
	2.6
per serving	1.3

Mix ingredients, using additional lemon juice and olive oil to thin dressing as desired. Let sit a few minutes. Pour over raw or cooked vegetables. Serves two.

Variation: Add 1 or 2 chopped anchovy fillets.

HOMEMADE MAYONNAISE

Make your own mayonnaise and omit both vinegar and sugar. Basic mayonnaise can be used alone or herbs may be added to make all sorts of dressings for salads, vegetables and fish.

Making mayonnaise is quite simple, although cookbooks caution about how it may curdle and offer remedies for rescuing it in such an event. As long as you drizzle the oil into the blender slowly while it whirs, you have no problem.

1 egg
2 tablespoons lemon juice
1 cup olive oil
1 teaspoon mustard, optional
¼ teaspoon powdered kelp, optional
¼ teaspoon salt, optional

CARBOHYDRATES	GRAMS
egg	.5
lemon juice	2.4
oil	trace
seasoning	1.7
	4.6

Beat egg in blender on low speed. Then add lemon juice and seasoning if desired. Continue to blend and slowly drizzle in oil. Continue blending until smooth. Makes 1½ to 2 cups. Stores for 2 to 3 days in the refrigerator.

CREAMY TOMATO DRESSING

2 tablespoons Homemade Mayonnaise (see above)
⅓ cup tomato, chopped
2 teaspoons lemon juice
⅛ teaspoon dried or 1 teaspoon fresh basil

CARBOHYDRATES	GRAMS
mayonnaise	.4
tomato	3.3
lemon juice	.8
	4.5

Blend on low speed in blender. Makes about ⅓ cup.

FRESH TOMATO DRESSING

1 cup tomatoes, chopped
2 tablespoons lemon juice
½ teaspoon kelp
1 clove garlic, minced
1 tablespoon fresh basil, oregano, or mint
⅛ teaspoon sea salt
½ teaspoon fresh horseradish, grated

CARBOHYDRATES	GRAMS
tomatoes	10.0
lemon	2.2
kelp, herbs	0.0
garlic	.9
horseradish	.2
	13.3

Blend on low speed in blender. Pour over salad greens. Makes ½ cup.

SAUCES

BUTTER-GINGER SAUCE

This sauce is especially good over fish, cooked carrots and zucchini.

2 tablespoons butter
1 cup onions, chopped
1 clove garlic, minced
1 teaspoon grated fresh ginger
2 teaspoons lemon juice (optional)

CARBOHYDRATES	GRAMS
butter	.1
onions	15.0
garlic	.9
ginger	1.3
lemon juice	.6
	17.9
per ⅓ cup serving	8.9

Simmer onions and garlic in butter until soft. Stir in ginger and lemon juice. Makes ⅔ cup.

CACCIATORE SAUCE

This sauce is good for fish, chicken, eggs and vegetables, especially zucchini and green beans.

1 tablespoon butter
½ cup onions, chopped
¼ cup green pepper, chopped
1½ cups tomato, chopped
½ cup parsley, chopped
1 tablespoon tomato paste (optional)
½ teaspoon dried basil or 1 tablespoon fresh basil leaves
½ teaspoon dried oregano or 1 tablespoon fresh oregano

CARBOHYDRATES	GRAMS
butter	.1
onions	7.5
green pepper	1.0
tomato	15.0
parsley	2.6
tomato paste	3.0
herbs	1.0
per ¾ cup	30.2

Melt butter over low heat. Add vegetables, tomato paste and herbs, and simmer until sauce is reduced to ¾ cup.

CURRY SAUCE

2 tablespoons butter
¼ cup onions, chopped
1 clove garlic, minced
1 inch piece ginger root, grated
¼ cup celery, chopped
¼ cup bell pepper, chopped
2 rounded tablespoons arrowroot
3 cups broth or soup stock seasoned to taste
1 tablespoon curry powder
seasoning salt to taste

CARBOHYDRATES	GRAMS
butter	.2
onions	3.7
ginger	1.3
garlic	0.9
celery	1.1
pepper	.9
arrowroot	14.0
curry	3.0
	25.1
per ½ cup serving	4.1

Melt butter over low heat. Add onions, garlic and ginger, and cook until softened. Add celery and bell pepper, cover and simmer for a few minutes. Mix arrowroot in ½ cup broth and stir into vegetables. Add remaining broth and heat, stirring over medium heat, until the mixture begins to boil. Reduce heat and simmer, stirring constantly, until sauce is clear and thick. Add curry powder and seasoning salt. Serve over rice, diced meats, vegetables, etc. Makes 3 cups.

MOCK HOLLANDAISE SAUCE

1 egg
¼ teaspoon seasoning salt
¼ teaspoon dulse or kelp
1 tablespoon lemon juice
½ stick butter (¼ cup)
¼ cup hot water

CARBOHYDRATES	GRAMS
egg	.5
lemon	1.2
butter	.4
1 cup	2.1
¼ cup serving	.5

Blend the first five ingredients until smooth. While blending on low speed, carefully add hot water. Stir over boiling water until thick. Makes about 1 cup.

ITALIAN MARINADE

3 tablespoons olive oil
3 tablespoons lemon juice
¼ tablespoon dried or 1 tablespoon fresh oregano
¼ teaspoon dried or 1 tablespoon fresh thyme
1 slice onion, optional
1 clove garlic, optional

CARBOHYDRATES	GRAMS
lemon juice	3.6
olive oil	0.0
herbs	0.0
onion	.6
garlic	.9
	5.1

Blend olive oil, lemon juice and herbs with a fork. Add onion and garlic. Makes about ⅓ cup.

LEMON MARINADE

6 tablespoons olive oil
3 tablespoons freshly squeezed lemon juice
3 tablespoons fresh parsley, chopped
1 tablespoon fresh chives, chopped
1 teaspoon onion, grated
1 clove garlic, minced
¼ teaspoon cumin seed, crushed
¼ teaspoon salt or kelp
⅛ teaspoon dry mustard

CARBOHYDRATES	GRAMS
lemon juice	3.6
parsley	1.0
chives	.5
onion	1.0
garlic	.9
herbs	.7
	7.7

Place all ingredients in small bowl or jar and stir or shake to mix well. Makes about ⅔ cup.

LEMON SAUCE

This delicate sauce can be made from your vegetable steaming water. (Avoid using steaming water with strongly flavored vegetables such as cabbage.)

1 tablespoon arrowroot
2 tablespoons cool water
1 teaspoon lemon rind, grated
1 egg yolk
2 tablespoons lemon juice
⅔ cup vegetable broth

CARBOHYDRATES	GRAMS
arrowroot	7.0
lemon rind	.3
lemon juice	2.4
egg yolk	.1
	9.8
per serving	4.9

Dissolve arrowroot and water in a small cup. Grate lemon rind and set aside. In a small bowl, beat egg yolk and lemon juice with fork. Add arrowroot mixture to vegetable broth and cook over medium heat until clear. Beat 3 tablespoons of this mixture, one after another, into lemon-egg yolk mixture and then combine with the rest of the vegetable broth. Add lemon rind. Simmer and stir constantly for 4 to 5 minutes. Makes about 1 cup.

Variations: Pour sauce over cauliflower, fish or chicken for a deliciously flavored dish.

QUICK ONION SAUCE

Onions can be used in a sauce to replace white or root vegetables in the Rainbow Meal Plan.

2 tablespoons butter
½ cup onions, chopped

CARBOHYDRATES	GRAMS
butter	**.2**
onions	**7.5**
	7.7
per serving	**3.9**

Melt butter over low heat. Simmer onions in butter until soft. Spoon over cooked vegetables, fish or brown rice. Serves two.

Variations: Add ½ cup finely minced parsley.
Add ½ teaspoon dried thyme or other favorite herbs, as desired.

SALSA DE LA COCINA

This is a good sauce to have available for fish or scrambled eggs. You can prepare it ahead and freeze it in small packages.

2 cups tomatoes or tomatillos, cut in pieces
1 small chili (½ if very hot) (optional)
1 cup cilantro (optional if available)
½ cup onions, chopped
½ cup bell pepper, chopped
½ teaspoon kelp
sea salt (to taste)

CARBOHYDRATES	GRAMS
tomatoes	**20.0**
chili	**.5**
cilantro	**3.0**
onions	**7.5**
bell pepper	**1.9**
kelp	**.9**
	33.8
per ¼ cup serving	**2.8**

Combine ingredients and serve, or chill if desired. Makes 3 cups, 12 quarter-cup servings.

Variations: Add ½ cup chopped parsley.
If cilantro is unavailable, add ½ teaspoon ground coriander seed.
For a different texture, you can puree ingredients at low speed in a blender briefly.

TARTAR SAUCE

½ cup Homemade Mayonnaise (see page 114)
1 to 2 tablespoons green onions or fresh chives
1 teaspoon lemon juice
1 teaspoon dried tarragon or 1 tablespoon fresh tarragon, scissor-snipped
1 teaspoon dried dill weed or 1 tablespoon fresh dill weed, scissor-snipped

CARBOHYDRATES	GRAMS
mayonnaise	**1.2**
green onions	**1.0**
lemon juice	**.3**
herbs	**.6**
	3.1
per serving	**1.5**

Mix with a fork and let sit while you prepare fish. Serves two.

Variation: Add 2 tablespoons finely chopped canned olives. Be sure to use a brand that has no additives.

CHEATS AND TREATS

We all cheat on occasion, but should not indulge too often. We should try to have rare splurges in the least harmful way possible. Some of the following suggestions stretch the health rules a little, but will offer something different for the occasional infraction of your diet.

Try a small handful of raw almonds or sunflower seeds. Soak them overnight to soften them. A combination of sunflower, pumpkin seeds and almonds is more textured and nutritious than the nuts or seeds by themselves.

Experiment with one-inch squares or thin slices of Essene Bread[22] (made from sprouted grain without yeast) toasted with butter. Limit your consumption of these goodies.

Make a batch of millet muffins. Indulge in one, and freeze the rest. Try the Sweet Potato Muffins.

Check the carbohydrate charts and choose the *least* harmful indulgences. If you crave fresh fruits, choose those with the lowest amounts of carbohydrates—for example, strawberries rather than bananas; or fresh or frozen strawberries with whipping cream rather than strawberry ice cream. (See Carbohydrate Chart, pages 136–140).

Above all, remember that your goal is renewed health. It is just not worthwhile to dig into the "sugar barrel." Keep patting yourself on the back mentally and encourage yourself by remembering how well you are doing. If you cheat, however, do not feel guilty. Forgive yourself, and continue with even greater resolve to adhere to the diet.

BAKED BEETS

This is an unusual dessert, and delicious.

1 medium or ½ large beet per person
whipped cream

CARBOHYDRATES	GRAMS
⅓ cup beets	**4.1**
cream	**.8**
per serving	**4.9**

Scrub the beets. Preheat oven to 375° F. Leave skins on. Bake in Pyrex baking dish for 45 minutes. Remove and allow the beets to cool just enough to handle with some old pot holder that is ready to be discarded. Grate the beets, using the large holes on the grater. (The skin will not go through the holes.) Place about ⅓ of grated beet in each sherbet glass, and top with ⅛ cup of whipped cream per serving.

Variation: Serve the cream, unwhipped, over the grated beets.

CARROT PUFF

It's pleasant to have a treat now and then! This is a good dessert dish for occasional use. The carrots are cooked a long time.

2 cups carrots, diced fine
2 tablespoons butter
1 cup onions, minced
1 egg, separated
¼ teaspoon salt
generous dash of powdered cloves

CARBOHYDRATES	GRAMS
carrots	**22.0**
butter	**.2**
onions	**15.0**
egg	**.5**
	37.7
per serving	**9.4**

Steam carrots until very tender, about 20 minutes. Melt butter over low heat and cook onion until tender. Preheat oven to 350° F. Puree carrots in blender or potato ricer (Foley mill). Add egg yolk and beat until smooth. In a small bowl, beat egg white until stiff, then fold into carrot mixture. Add salt and cloves. Turn mixture into buttered 5 × 9-inch glass loaf pan and bake 20 to 25 minutes. Serve hot with a lemon wedge. Serves four.

JELL TREAT

1 cup hot water
2 heaping teaspoons Dacopa*[22]
1 heaping tablespoon unflavored gelatin
ice cubes
Fake Cream for topping (optional) (see
    below)

CARBOHYDRATES	GRAMS
	negligible

Make a jell by mixing hot water, Dacopa and gelatin in the blender at low speed. Drop ice cubes one at a time into the blender, while continuing to blend until jelled. Serve with or without Fake Cream. Serves two or three.

*Dahlia tuber coffee substitute or other coffee substitute made without malt or fruit. Found in health/natural food stores.

FAKE CREAM

When good quality whipping cream (raw certified or pasteurized with no additives—not Ultra Pasteurized) is unavailable, try this substitute.

1 cup hot (near boiling) pure water
2 rounded tablespoons of pure unflavored
    gelatin (vegetable gelatin if you can find
    it, called agar-agar)
1 stick (½ cup) unsalted butter
3 eggs
1 tablespoon pure almond or vanilla extract*
ice cubes

CARBOHYDRATES	GRAMS
butter	**.8**
eggs	**1.5**
	2.3

*Bickford's pure extracts are made from herbs, foods and spices, in a corn oil base. Find them in health/natural food stores.

Pour water into the blender. Slowly add gelatin and blend at low speed. Add butter, eggs and flavoring, continuing to blend. As blender whirs, add ice cubes one at a time through the inner lid, until the mixture jells. Makes a generous quart of Fake Cream.

Variations: Use as a base for eggnog or as a cereal topping. Drop frozen berries into the mixture, instead of ice cubes, to make an instant fruit ice cream.

SWEET POTATO SOUFFLÉ

3 small steamed sweet potatoes
3 eggs, separated
¼ cup pure water, boiling
1 tablespoon unflavored gelatin
1 teaspoon pumpkin pie spice mix
½ cup whipped cream or Fake Cream (see above)

CARBOHYDRATES	GRAMS
sweet potatoes	**111.0**
eggs	**1.5**
gelatin	**0.0**
spice	**.5**
	113.0
per serving	**18.8**

Steam sweet potatoes and blend, rice or mash to produce about 2 cups pulp. Separate eggs. Place water in blender, turn on low speed and add gelatin. Gradually add egg yolks, pumpkin pie spice and sweet potato pulp while continuing to blend into puree. Chill. It will form a firm custard. Serve in sherbet glasses. Top with whipped cream or Fake Cream. Makes six ½ cup servings.

*B*EVERAGES

There is no universal agreement as to what type of potable water is best, but most experts agree that ordinarily tap water should be avoided. In the recipes, we refer both to cooking and drinking water, and suggest the use of distilled, spring, purified, filtered water, or water treated by reverse osmosis. For the average person the total daily quantity should be from six to eight glasses, spaced throughout the day.

Water from the steamer pot contains minerals leached from cooking. This liquid can be saved for broths rather than thrown away.

Sparkling waters, especially mineral waters, are enjoyable with a twist of lemon or lime.

Herb teas are popular but may contain molds. Their use depends on individual tolerances. Many use Pau d'Arco (taheebo) tea. It is reported to have anti-fungal properties. Other teas with similar qualities include chamomile, bergamot, hyssop, alfalfa, angelica root and lemon grass.

Avoid coffee, nonherbal tea and artificially sweetened beverages. Try the beverages in this cookbook and experiment on your own.

EGGNOG

This is an ideal beverage to take with any vitamin or mineral powders your doctor has prescribed.

1 egg in blender along with ¼ cup Fake Cream (see page 124) or 1 tablespoon cream	**CARBOHYDRATES** GRAMS
	egg **.5**
3 tablespoons water	Fake Cream **.1**
	.6

Blend quickly.

Variation: For a brisk flavor, add 4 fresh mint leaves.

LEMON-CINNAMON TEA

2 sticks cinnamon
2 cups water
juice and peel of ½ lemon

CARBOHYDRATES	GRAMS
lemon juice and peel	**2.9**
per serving	**.7**

Place cinnamon in water in saucepan and cook over low heat. After steeping about 15 minutes, add the juice and peel of lemon. Steep without heat, but covered, another 5 minutes. Serves four.

LEMON TRILOGY TEA

1 teaspoon each of lemon grass, lemon balm
and lemon verbena
1 quart water

CARBOHYDRATES	GRAMS
	negligible

Prepare as herb tea or steeped tea.

Variations: If you have a lemon tree, use 1 or 2 leaves from it as well. A blossom or two from any citrus tree adds greatly to the fragrance of this brew.

MINT-FLAVORED CAFE

This was grandmother's remedy for disturbed digestion. Many a stomachache was feigned to obtain the remedy!

1 cup dandelion or chicory tea
2 to 4 drops oil of peppermint

CARBOHYDRATES	GRAMS
	negligible

Pour a cup of boiling water over a tablespoon of dandelion or chicory tea or a handful of fresh leaves, cover tightly and steep for 10 to 20 minutes. Add peppermint and stir.

PEPPERMINT TEA

1 handful of mint leaves or ½ cup dried mint leaves
1 quart water

CARBOHYDRATES GRAMS
negligible

Chop a handful of mint leaves and cover with 1 quart hot water, or take ¼ cup dried mint leaves and soak 6 hours in a quart of water. Strain. Heat to serving temperature, if desired.

Variation: Place either fresh or dried mint and water in the blender and whirl, then strain. Serves four.

SPARKLING HERB TEA

2 tablespoons dried herbs or ⅓ cup fresh
1 quart pure water
ice made with pure water
1 quart sparkling water
lemon slices (optional)

CARBOHYDRATES GRAMS
negligible

Add any favorite herbs or combination of herbs to water and simmer in a covered pot for 20 minutes. Let tea cool to room temperature. Pour into quart jar, cover and chill 1 to 2 hours. Put ice cubes in glasses. Fill glasses half full with tea, and the remainder with sparkling water. Drop 1 lemon slice into each glass. Makes 8 eight-ounce servings.

Eating Out

Prepare your own food as much as possible. Use frozen left-overs you have prepared for emergencies when pressed for time. A tempting alternative to dining out is to treat yourself to an expensive cut of meat or fish you ordinarily would not buy and prepare it at home to accompany your favorite vegetables.

Often, dining out is unavoidable. When this occurs, make the best of it if you aren't going to cheat. It is hoped that you will be dining at a good restaurant where food is prepared fresh daily on the premises. Choose plain foods. Avoid those with sauces that are apt to contain sugar and vinegar. If they are tasty, you are tempted to overeat. Order the foods to which you have become accustomed, such as prime rib, roast chicken or baked, poached or broiled fish. Avoid charcoal-grilled foods and rolled deli meats. Share a baked potato with a friend.

Order Perrier with a wedge of lime and make it a festive occasion. Request a vegetable relish plate, try vegetable dishes à la carte, or select a homemade clear (not cream) soup with vegetables.

Sip a cup of herbal tea (carry your own tea bag) or simply flavor a cup of steaming hot water with lemon. Above all, make the event enjoyable.

A Menu Sampler

Breakfast

Measure servings carefully since it is difficult to gauge ¼-cup size portions initially. Take care to consult the carbohydrate charts if in doubt. Your basic breakfast consists of 1 part protein, 1 part starch and 5 parts vegetables. Some suggested substitutes for cereals in the following menus are:

> Freshly ground cream of rye, oats, rice
> Steamed wholegrain wheat, barley, millet, oats
> Sweet potato or other tuber pancakes

A "hurry-up" breakfast may include:

> eggnog
> sweet potato muffin
> choice of 4 raw vegetables

BREAKFAST I

1 serving flaxseed cereal with ⅛ cup heavy cream
¼ cup portions each of:
> broiled fish
> steamed chard
> steamed peas
> raw carrot
> raw celery
> raw tomato

BREAKFAST II

1 serving cream of grain (wheat) cereal with butter
broiled lamb kidneys
¼ cup portion each of:
> steamed asparagus
> steamed beets
> raw watercress
> raw cucumber
> raw bell pepper

BREAKFAST III

1 serving psyllium seed cereal
⅛ cup heavy cream
Spanish omelet, 1 serving

BREAKFAST IV

1 serving steamed wholegrain rye cereal
¼ cup portions each of:
> poached egg on steamed beet greens
> steamed beets
> raw celery
> raw zucchini, and broccoli flowerets

BREAKFAST V

1 serving oat bran cereal with heavy cream
¼ cup portion each of:
> broiled steak
> steamed celery with edible pea pods
> raw turnip slices, parsley sprigs and cherry tomatoes

BREAKFAST VI

¼ of oat bran waffle and butter
¼ cup portion each of:
> lamb sausage
> steamed broccoli and celery
> raw carrots, radishes and lettuce

Lunch

Luncheon ideas include soups or stews, salads, raw vegetables with dips, or cooked vegetables. Some cold cooked meats, fish or fowl are tasty. These, as well as your favorite egg dishes, can be served steaming hot.

LUNCH I

turkey hash
salad

LUNCH II

Italian fish stew
salad

LUNCH III

broiled chicken
Caesar salad

LUNCH IV

tostadas
raw vegetables

LUNCH V

steak salad
mug of hot broth

LUNCH VI

fish salad
mug of hot mint tea

Remember to use ¼-cup servings except when the dish consists of a mixture. Then multiply the ¼ cup by the vegetables and protein in the recipe. Repeat the process for dinners.

Dinner

DINNER I

roast turkey and gravy
stove top holiday dressing
green salad

DINNER II

lamb kabobs
mint-pea salad

DINNER III

cooked tongue
steamed broccoli
assorted raw vegetables

DINNER IV

poached fish
asparagus and hollandaise
   sauce
kasha
coleslaw

DINNER V

broiled beefsteak
crowned eggplant
carrot-cabbage salad

DINNER VI

vegetable-beef soup
millet muffin
assorted raw vegetables

DINNER VII

fish in butter-ginger sauce
small baked potato
steamed string beans
raw tomato, romaine lettuce and cucumber
anchovy dressing

Candida Folk Wisdom

Garlic is said to be anti-fungal. Many people suffering from Candida claim to feel better when using more garlic than the ordinary amount used as spicy seasoning. The simple way to extract garlic oil for concentrated use is with alcohol such as vodka.

Ingredients:
½ pound peeled garlic cloves
1 bottle (fifth or quart) vodka or gin

Place the garlic cloves in the blender with 1 cup of alcohol. Blend the mixture until it becomes mush. Add a second cup of alcohol and blend. Pour into a quart jar. Rinse the blender with ⅓ cup of alcohol and add this to the jar. Cap the jar with a firm-sealing lid that cannot leak. Shake the jar daily just long enough to mix well. Repeat this procedure for 10 days. Each day thereafter check the jar for about 1 inch of garlic oil rising to the top. Remove the oil by gently skimming or pouring. Don't use any of the mash sediment.

Collect the oil in an eye-dropper bottle and use as seasoning or external remedy. It is delicious blended into softened butter to top vegetables, or in the salad dressing. Each time oil is removed, add a little alcohol to the jar. When no more oil rises, discard the mush and make a new batch.

Taheebo or Pau d'Arco Tea

This tea has apparently helped many Candida patients. The tea is made from inner tree bark and imported from South America.

It is brewed as follows:
1 heaping tablespoon tea or the contents of three tea bags, emptied into pot
1 quart water

Add the water to the tea and simmer on the lowest heat possible for at least half an hour. Allow the liquid to cool and pour into a storage jar with a tight-sealing lid. Refrigerate, and sip the chilled tea as desired. Adjust the recipe to make enough to be completely consumed in two days.

Foods for the Yeast-Sensitive to Avoid

Yeast is found in all manufactured citric acid and in most fruits; in vinegar, which is made of fermented wines, and in ciders from such fruits as grapes, pears, apples and some herbs. Vinegar is used as a preservative for mustard, catsup, olives, mayonnaise, many dressings, pickles, horseradish, spices, soy sauce, Worcestershire sauce and dried fruits. Canned or frozen fruit juices contain yeast; only hand-squeezed and fresh juices are yeast-free. Fruit and fruit products that are canned commercially have a higher yeast content than those that are canned at home. Melons (especially cantaloupe) and oranges are loaded with molds and yeast on the outside skins. Fruits should be peeled, not cut into, because in the motion of cutting through the skin with a knife, the meat of the fruit is contaminated.

Mushrooms and cheeses of all kinds contain or actually are specific types of molds or yeasts; for instance, Roquefort cheese contains the mold *Penicillium roqueforti*. Other yeast-containing milk products are buttermilk, sour cream, cream cheese, ricotta cheese, ice creams, powdered milks and milk itself.

Tea, pepper, coffee, coffee substitutes, many spices and tobacco acquire molds or yeast in their drying processes. Leftovers from a previous meal should be frozen for future use, as they will become mold-containing within twenty-four hours. Brown spots on any food are yeasts and molds that have begun their job of breaking down that food's nutrients for their own survival. Vitamins, such as the B-complex thiamine, niacin and riboflavin are usually yeast-grown, although it is possible to obtain them with a brown rice base, yeast-free. Antibiotics such as penicillin, mycin drugs, tetracyclines, linococin and chloromycetin are derived from mold cultures.

Malt is used as a flavoring and coloring agent; it is the major ingredient of beer, ale and malt liquors, as well as some nonalcoholic products. Malt is a sprouted grain, easily fermented, and produces the enzyme diastase, important in the development of grain liquors. Most dry breakfast cereals contain malt or malt extract—Grape-Nuts is exceptionally high in malt content.

Other foods which encourage Candida albicans are baked

goods, breads, biscuits and pancake mixes, soda crackers and any other foods requiring the use of baker's yeast. Ice cream, candy, malted milk drinks and soda fountain drinks contain sugar yeast.

This information is used with the kind permission of John A. Henderson, M.D., E.N.T. *Surgery and Allergy*, San Diego, CA, 1984.

Carbohydrates and Calories

This list has been abbreviated to refer to the anti-fungal diet. Some additional foods to augment the diet have been added. Care should be taken, as the body chemistry improves and symptoms become less severe, to experiment with caution.

The figures have been drawn from:

Nutritive Value of Foods, Science and Education Administration, Home and Garden Bulletin Number 72.

Composition of Foods, Agriculture Handbook Number 8, Agricultural Research Service, U.S.D.A.

For further information on expanded dietary needs consult:

Nutrition Almanac, Nutrition Search Inc. New York: McGraw-Hill.

Composition and Facts about Foods, Ford Heritage, Health Research, PO Box 70, Mokelumne Hill, CA 95245.

Where figures are not available from the U.S. Government publications, the numbers given are approximate.

Foods noted with an asterisk are those to be added judiciously to the diet when tolerated.

	PORTION	CARBS (GRAMS)	CALORIES
*almonds	¼ cup	6.9	
	1 cup	27.7	600
*arrowroot	1 cup	112.0	
	1 T	7.0	
artichoke, globe	1 cup	10.6	9–47
artichoke, Jerusalem	½ cup	16.7	50
asparagus	1 cup	5.0	30
avocado	1	12.6	334
baking powder	1 t	2.0	5
	1 T	7.0	
bamboo shoots, 4 spears		2.0	10
barley	¼ cup	19.0	150

	PORTION	CARBS (GRAMS)	CALORIES
beans:			
*black-eyed peas	1 cup	35.0	190
*garbanzos	1 cup dry	122.0	720
	1 cup cooked	60.0	360
green snap, cooked	½ cup	4.0	25
raw	1 cup	7.0	30
*kidney, cooked	1 cup	42.0	238
*lima	1 cup	35.0	190
*pinto, cooked	1 cup	60.5	330
beets:			
cooked, whole	2 (2″)	7.0	30
cooked, sliced or diced	1 cup	13.5	55
beverages:			
carbonated water		0.0	0
club soda		0.0	0
Perrier	1 bottle	0.0	0
*blackberries	1 cup	19.0	85
*blueberries	1 cup	22.0	90
bok choy, cooked	1 cup	4.0	25
raw	1 cup	7.0	40
broccoli, cooked	1 cup	7.0	40
brussels sprouts, cooked	1 cup	10.0	55
*bulgur, cooked	1 cup	85.0	420
dry	1 cup	129.0	602
butter, ¼ lb.	½ cup	.8	814
cabbage:			
cooked	1 cup	6.0	30
Chinese	1 cup	2.0	10
raw, shredded (red and white)	1 cup	5.0	20
cacciatore sauce	1 cup	40.0	
carbonated water		0.0	0
carob	½ cup	58.4	112
	1 T	7.3	16
carrot, cooked	1 cup	11.0	50
grated	1 cup	11.0	45
raw	7¼ × ⅛″	7.0	30
cauliflower	1 cup	6.0	31
celeriac	½ cup	8.5	40

	PORTION	CARBS (GRAMS)	CALORIES
celery, 1 stalk	8 " × 1½"	2.0	5
chopped	1 cup	4.7	
leaves chopped	1 cup	5.0	
chayote, diced	1 cup	5.0	20
chicken livers	1 cup	8.2	
chives	¾ cup	6.0	28
cilantro	½ cup	1.0	
corn, 1 ear	5' × 1¾"	16.0	79
*kernels, cooked	1 cup	31.0	130
corn meal, grits			
*cooked	1 cup	27.0	125
*uncooked	1 cup	90.0	435
cucumber	1¾" × 1	1.0	5
diced	1 cup	3.6	16
dandelion greens, cooked	1 cup	7.0	35
egg, large	1	.5	80
eggplant, steamed	1 cup	7.40	34
cooked	1 large	18–20	100
endive, raw	1 cup	2.0	10
fish, fowl, meats		0.0	
garlic	1 clove	.9	4
ginger root	1 ounce	2.6	
gelatin	1 T	0.0	25
*grapefruit	½	13.0	50
greens, cooked			
beet	1 cup	5.0	25
collard	1 cup	10.0	65
mustard	1 cup	6.0	30
turnip	1 cup	5.0	30
herbs, most		0.0	0
horseradish	1 t	0.5	2
jicama	1 cup	25.6	
kale, cooked	1 cup	7.0	45
lemon juice	1 T	1.0	4
*lentils, cooked	1 cup	39.0	210

	PORTION	CARBS (GRAMS)	CALORIES
lettuce			
Boston	5" head	4.0	25
iceberg	6" head	12.5	70
looseleaf, chopped	1 cup	2.0	10
lime juice	1 cup	22.0	65
mayonnaise	1 cup	2.6	1600
	1 T	.06	100
millet, cooked	1 cup	56.0	248
dry	1 cup	166.0	746
mustard	1 t	0.0	5
nuts:			
*Brazil	3 oz.	7.5	400
*filberts	1 cup	19.0	730
*macadamia	½ cup	15.9	691
*pecans	1 cup	17.0	816
*pine nuts	½ cup	12.0	550
*walnuts	1 cup	19.0	780
oat bran	1/3 cup	16.0	110
oatmeal, cooked	1 cup	23.0	130
oils		0.0	
okra, 3" × ⅝"	10 pods	6.0	30
olives, ripe	3 small, 2 large	0.1	15
onions:			
chopped	1 cup	15.0	65
sliced	1 cup	10.0	45
*papaya, cubed	1 cup	14.0	55
parsley, chopped	1 cup	5.0	trace
parsnips	1 cup	23.0	100
peas, cooked	1 cup	19.0	110
peapods or snowpeas	½ cup	24.0	
peppers, sweet, raw	1	4.9	15
chopped	½ cup	1.9	
potatoes:			
*diced	1 cup	25.7	114
*baked	1 8 oz.	33.0	145
*boiled	1 5 oz.	23.0	105
*sweet, baked	1 6½ oz.	37.0	160
boiled	1 6½ oz.	40.0	170

	PORTION	CARBS (GRAMS)	CALORIES
*popcorn, popped	1 cup	5.0	25
*pumpkin seeds	1 cup	21.0	775
radishes, raw	4	1.0	5
*raspberries	1 cup	13.0	55
rice:			
brown			
cooked	1 cup	37.0	178
raw	1 cup	161.0	744
wild	1 cup	30.0	145
flour	1 cup	85.0	270
rutabaga, cooked	1 cup	15.4	64
sliced, raw	1 cup	13.9	60
rye, wholegrain	1 cup	68	330
scallions, chopped	1 cup	8.2	36
sesame seeds	1 cup	26.4	873
shallots, chopped	1 cup	27.2	112
sunflower seeds	1 cup	28.9	812
spinach, chopped			
cooked	1 cup	6.0	40
raw	1 cup	2.0	15
squash, cooked			
summer	1 cup	7.0	30
*winter, mashed	1 cup	32.0	130
*strawberries	1 cup	13.0	55
*taro, tuber	½ cup	24.0	98
tomatoes:			
raw	4 oz.	6.0	25
canned, no citric acid			
fresh, chopped	1 cup	10.0	50
tomato paste	1 T	3.0	13
tortillas, corn	1	13.5	
turnips, diced	1 cup	8.0	35
watercress	1 cup	2.2	
*watermelon	4″ × 8″ wedge	27.0	110
wheat, whole	1 cup	34.0	85
whipping cream	1 cup	7.0	700–800
zucchini, chopped	1 cup	5.5	

References

1. C. Orian Truss, M.D., *The Missing Diagnosis* (Birmingham, Alabama: P.O. Box 26508, Birmingham, 35226, 1983).

2. C. Orian Truss, M.D., "The Role of Candida Albicans in Human Illness," *Journal of Orthomolecular Psychiatry* vol. 10, no. 4 (1981).

3. *William G. Crook, M.D., *The Yeast Connection* (Jackson, Tennessee: Professional Books, 1984).

4. *Weston A. Price, D.D.S., *Nutrition and Physical Degeneration* (La Mesa, California: Price-Pottenger Nutrition Foundation, 1970).

5. *Melvin E. Page, D.D.S., and H. Leon Abrams, Jr., *Your Body Is Your Best Doctor* (New Canaan, Connecticut: Keats Publishing, 1972).

6. †Shirley Lorenzani, Ph.D., article reprints included in Candida Reprints *Candida Albicans, Friend or Foe* (La Mesa, California: Price-Pottenger Nutrition Foundation, 1984).

7. William G. Crook, M.D., *The Yeast Connection.*

8. James Beard, *The Theory and Practice of Good Cooking* (New York: Alfred A. Knopf, 1977).

9. Clara Felix, *The Felix Letter* (Berkeley, California, P.O. Box 7094, 94754, 1983): vol. 16.

10. Jeffrey Bland, Ph.D., *Digestive Enzymes*, (New Canaan, Connecticut: Keats Publishing, 1983).
    James W. Anderson, M.D., Veterans Administration Medical Center, Lexington, KY 40511, *The American Journal of Clinical Nutrition* 34 (May 1981).

11. *Pat Connolly, *Guide to Living Foods* (La Mesa, California: Price-Pottenger Nutrition Foundation, 1978).

12. Brenner Stainless Steel, 1741 North Ivar, Office 90028, Suite 111, or P.O. Box 549, Hollywood, California 90078.

13. Adelle Davis, *Let's Cook It Right* (New York: New American Library, 1970).

†Shirley Lorenzani, Ph.D., Cassette Tapes, Sets I and II (La Mesa, California: Price-Pottenger Nutrition Foundation, 1978).

14. *Melvin E. Page, D.D.S., and H. Leon Abrams, Jr., *Your Body Is Your Best Doctor.*

15. Adelle Davis, *Let's Cook It Right.*

16. Beatrice Trum Hunter, *The Natural Foods Primer* (New York: Simon and Schuster, 1972).

17. James Beard, *Theory and Practice of Good Cooking.*

18. James Beard, *Fish Cookery* (New York: Warner Books 1967).

19. Irma S. Rombauer and Marion Rombauer Becker, *Joy of Cooking* (Indianapolis: Bobbs Merrill, 1967).

20. *Francis M. Pottenger, Jr., M.D., *Pottenger's Cats* (La Mesa, California: Price-Pottenger Nutrition Foundation, 1983).

21. James Beard, *Theory and Practice of Good Cooking,*

22. Essene Bread, made of sprouted grains and yeast-free ingredients, can be found in your health food store or ordered from distributors: on the West Coast, California Natural Foods Products, Mateca, California 95336; East Coast, Stowmills, P.O. Box 816, Brattleboro, Vermont 05301.

*Items noted may be ordered from the PRICE-POTTENGER NUTRITION FOUNDATION, POST OFFICE BOX NUMBER 2614, LA MESA, CALIFORNIA 92041

Index

HOW CAN I HELP?

PRICE-POTTENGER NUTRITION FOUNDATION invites you to JOIN NOW!

We are a non-profit educational organization; all contributions and dues are tax-deductible.

We trust that you will benefit from the carefully planned diet included herein. When you, as many others have, indicate a desire to help further the work of the Foundation, we urge you to contribute. Please inform others who might also like to take part in facilitating our services to Candida patients.

PRICE-POTTENGER NUTRITION FOUNDATION
P.O. BOX 2614, LA MESA, CALIFORNIA